Roy's
fish & seafood

Roy Yamaguchi
with John Harrisson

Roy's®

fish & seafood

Recipes from the Pacific Rim

Fish, seafood, and
location photography by
John De Mello

Food photography by
Scott Peterson

TEN SPEED PRESS
Berkeley | Toronto

To the late Tom and Warren Matsuda,
        to all fishermen, and to those who love fish.

Ten Speed Press
Box 7123
Berkeley, California 94707
www.tenspeed.com

Distributed in Australia by Simon and Schuster Australia, in Canada by Ten Speed Press Canada,
in New Zealand by Southern Publishers Group, in South Africa by Real Books, and in the United Kingdom
and Europe by Airlift Book Company.

Cover and text design by Toni Tajima
Food styling by Roy Yamaguchi, Karen Shinto, and John Sikhattana
Prop styling by Emma Star Jensen

Thank you to the following people and organizations for their contributions to the fish, seafood, and location
shots: Mike Straight at Maggie Joe; Glenn Tanoue, president of Tropic Fish; Jo Rasmussen, sales representative at Tropic Fish; Honolulu Fish Auction and the United Fishing Agency; Romy's Kahuku Prawns and
Shrimp; Kapono Zukevich; James Ashe of Waiale'e Fisheries for the Kona crab and lobster; and Nishimoto
Fish Market.

Library of Congress Cataloging-in-Publication Data on file with the publisher.

ISBN 10: 1-58008-482-6
ISBN 13: 978-1-58008-482-6

Printed in China
First printing, 2005

1 2 3 4 5 6 7 8 9 10 — 09 08 07 06 05

contents

acknowledgments

my thanks to the following individuals—and friends—who helped make this book a reality:

Gordon Hopkins, Partner/Director of Chefs at Roy's, and David Abella, Roy's Corporate Chef, who contributed recipes; Joey Macadangdang, Executive Chef and Greg Ritchie, Chef/Partner at Orlando, who also developed recipes for this book; the other chefs at Roy's who helped test the recipes and contributed to the creative process; John Sikhattana, Chef/Partner at Roy's in San Francisco, for his help with the food photography; Jo "JoJo" Rasmussen at Tropic Fish for her part in refining my learning process over the years and for helping organize the Hawaii photo shoot; Howard Deese, marine programs specialist in the Ocean Resources Branch of the State of Hawaii Department of Business, Economic Development and Tourism, for his dedication in providing information on Hawaiian seafood to a wide audience; Brooks Takenaka, assistant auction manager with the United Fishing Agency, which runs the Honolulu Fish Auction, for making it "da bes';"and Dean Okimoto at Nalo Farms for his fresh produce that always inpsires great dishes.

Robbyn Shim for organizing and typing drafts of the recipes; John Harrisson for putting everything together, as usual; Rainer Kumbroch, who joined me for late night meals as the manuscript was taking shape.

Phil Wood at Ten Speed Press for believing in my cookbook ambitions; Toni Tajima, for the book's design; Scott Peterson, for the food photography; Karen Shinto, for the food styling; Emma Star Jensen for the prop styling; John De Mello for the fish, seafood, and location photography; and Carrie Rodrigues, my editor at Ten Speed, for the fine-tuning.

introduction

fish and seafood are the backbone of the menu at each and

every Roy's restaurant. After all, the rich bounty of the ocean that surrounds us is one of the main elements that distinguish Hawaiian cuisine from that of most other regions. We are particularly blessed here in the islands to have so many wonderful and spectacular species of fish available year-round, and if it's fresh fish you crave, it's hard to imagine a better location anywhere else in the world. This precious resource is now appearing more than ever before on menus in restaurants and hotel dining rooms across the islands, and Pacific seafood is becoming more and more popular on mainland menus.

I was born and raised in Japan, and my family's diet was pretty typical in featuring plenty of fish. Every other year, we would travel to Hawaii to visit relatives, and one of the first stops my parents would make in Honolulu was to buy fish and shellfish at Tamashiro Market (which is still a culinary landmark) so we could cook it at home. Some of my earliest food memories involved fish and seafood, and having lived in Hawaii for many years now, I have a particular affinity and respect for the wonderful world-class seafood available here. I enjoy deep-sea sportfishing, like many Hawaiians. Fishing with lines and nets gives us a real connection to the ocean and the traditions and history of the island on which we live.

At Roy's, I am always being asked about Hawaiian fish, especially by guests visiting from the mainland and beyond. After all, the names—onaga, nairagi, and shutome—are often a mystery, even if the fish themselves (snapper, marlin, and swordfish) are familiar. This is one of the reasons for this cookbook, which in part serves as a guide to describe the main types of Pacific fish and seafood, especially those enjoyed in Hawaii. Sections on each type of fish or seafood offer close substitutions and alternatives for readers who live in other parts of the country. This book is also a collection of almost one hundred recipes featuring Pacific seafood that I have adapted for preparation in the home kitchen. Many of these recipes draw on ingredients, techniques, and traditions from all across the Pacific, reflecting Hawaii's diverse population and the culinary influences to which it is happily exposed. They also reflect my own Hawaiian Fusion style of cooking: This is based on the freshest local ingredients—especially seafood—bold Asian spices, European (and especially French)-influenced sauces and techniques, together with Pan-Pacific and Hawaiian traditions.

The availability and use of Pacific fish and seafood have not always been as widespread, even here in the Hawaiian Islands. As recently as the 1980s, the saying went that the best food tourists were likely to enjoy on a trip to Hawaii was the in-flight meal. Most of the ingredients used in hotel dining rooms and restaurants were flown in from the mainland and beyond. Often, the fish was frozen, and because so many of the chefs were European, the types of seafood that were most familiar came all the way from Europe, on the other side of the world. Happily, all this changed with the development of Hawaii Regional Cuisine by a group of a dozen or so young and talented island chefs in the late 1980s and early 1990s, and their subsequent encouragement of local suppliers and growers. I was fortunate to be a member of this group, and now, together with a whole new generation of chefs, we continue to make the most of our island resources, and to work with innovative individuals to establish new products locally.

These positive developments apply equally to the variety and quality of fresh fish and seafood that consumers and restaurateurs enjoy here in Hawaii and beyond. I have learned a lot by working with my main Honolulu seafood supplier, Tropic Fish (see page 236), one of several excellent sources that I can recommend. It helps that Honolulu's fish auction—the wholesale market for the commercial catch, and one of the most important markets of its kind in the United States—are held early every morning, six days a week. Tuna and swordfish account for the largest part of the tonnage that changes hands at the auction, but just about every other type of Pacific fish, both open-water and bottom fish (but not reef fish), are landed here. Due in part to this accessibility, as well as to custom and eating habits, Hawaiians consume twice as much seafood compared to the national average.

The tradition of fish and seafood consumption in Hawaii goes back to the first Polynesian settlers, who arrived in the archipelago thousands of years ago. In ancient Hawaiian society, fishing provided most of the protein in peoples' diet, although sea-food was consumed mainly as a side dish to accompany the main staple starch (taro, poi, breadfruit, or sweet potato); land-based agriculture was well advanced, providing a balanced diet. Typically, seafood was eaten raw, dried, fermented, baked, and broiled. Ancient Hawaiians also engaged in aquaculture, creating both freshwater and saltwater fishponds to cultivate fish, most notably moi, destined for consumption by the ali'i, or nobility. In addition to songs and chants honoring the harvest of the sea, there are many ancient Hawaiian fishing legends that celebrate the most successful fishermen and their exploits, and these have been handed down through the generations. These tales echo traditional cultural values, especially the importance of conserving and sharing the supply of fish and seafood.

There are lessons about the sustainability of ocean resources that we can learn from the ancient Hawaiians. The ali'i used kapu—prohibitions—to restrict fishing in certain areas and seasons, especially during spawning. When open-ocean fishing was restricted, inshore and reef fishing was permitted, and vice versa. The kapu system was not arbitrary but followed patterns of nature. The system of distribution of the fishing harvest (hukilau) took into account not only the ali'i's share, but also that of those who had set the nets made from native fibers and vines, paddled the canoes, and helped land the fish. The major portion of the catch was kept by the fishermen.

Over recent decades, as the healthfulness and excellent eating qualities of fish have become increasingly appreciated, the problem of overfishing has grown. Some recent reports point to destructive fishing practices that have reduced worldwide stocks by at least 90 percent over the past few decades. The average size of the catch is much reduced in most oceans, and the depletion of mature breeding fish stocks is compounding and accelerating the problem. Some governments and international agencies are beginning to take protective action, but many believe it is too little, too late.

Occasionally, overfishing is the result of culinary trends, such as the demand for Cajun blackened redfish in the 1980s. Until then, redfish was a common and affordable Gulf fish, but following the sudden huge demand, it is now scarce and legally protected. In the Northeast and off Canada's Grand Banks fishing grounds, cod and haddock are now endangered; in Europe, North Sea cod and sole are likewise threatened; in South America, Chilean sea bass has become seriously depleted. On the East coast of the United States, lobster and oysters were the food of the "common people" in the nineteenth century, but overharvesting and a revised appreciation for these seafoods have made them much more expensive. Fortunately, they have not been overexploited to the point of disappearing, like some fish stocks, but we must take care not to mortgage the future of generations that follow. This is a principle close to the heart of the ancient Hawaiian culture, and I encourage you to follow this example by supporting national and local initiatives supporting sustainable fishery policies (as well as sustainable agricultural practices). During the 1980s, the public outcry over tuna fishing led to "dolphin-friendly" nets and fishing practices, and perhaps it is time to raise public awareness and consciousness of today's issues of depletion in a similar way to ensure that the invaluable resource of our oceans is safeguarded.

notes on buying and storing fish and seafood

patronize a reputable fishmonger if

at all possible, and don't be shy about asking questions about the types of fish, where they were caught, and their freshness. Knowing your supplier will give you a tremendous advantage in terms of quality and protecting yourself from health issues. Fresh fish are usually preferable to frozen and thawed, which means buying varieties that are in season (this suggestion applies equally well to other produce). The good news is that many types of fish and seafood are available fresh most of the year, although you should keep in mind that some "fresh" fish may have been on board a fishing boat for longer than fish that has been flash frozen immediately. There are no absolute rules—just use your common sense and some of the guidelines described below, and be prepared to be flexible when shopping for fish. If necessary, buy a similar type of fish as a substitute. If purchasing seafood at a supermarket, talk to the manager of the fish department and try to establish a relationship as a regular (and knowledgeable) customer. If you are not satisfied with the cleanliness or aroma of the fish store or fish department, buy elsewhere.

In selecting fish, make sure there is no "fishy" aroma or ammonia-type odor; fresh fish should smell fresh, like seawater. Whole fish should appear shiny, the gills should be bright red, and the eyes should be clear; if they are cloudy, or sunken, the fish is not fresh. Any natural coloration should appear vivid. The scales and fins should be tightly formed, undamaged, and intact. Ask the fishmonger to clean and scale whole fish for you, and if this is not possible, do so yourself as soon as possible to prevent decay or spoilage. Whole fish, fillets, and steaks should have a uniform color and not show blemishes or areas of discoloration. When you get the fish home, touch it; it should feel firm and elastic, and not soft or flabby. Lobsters, crab, and shrimp may be purchased in live or cooked form, but all other shellfish sold in the shell should be live. Here's a helpful tip: I always carry a small cooler in my car trunk so that, in case I buy fish on an impulse, I can keep it cool until I get home. If I have preplanned to buy fish, I put a couple of frozen ice packs in the cooler before I set off.

Wrap fresh fish and shellfish in damp paper towels or a damp cloth to prevent from drying out and place in the coldest part of the refrigerator, or store over ice, as soon after purchase as possible. Use it as soon as you can, preferably the same day; it will progressively lose its freshness otherwise. When preparing fish and shellfish, keep work surfaces and utensils clean and wash them, as well as your hands, afterward.

When cooking fish, check constantly for doneness; many types of seafood will dry out and become tough if overcooked. In general, fish should feel firm yet tender and not tough when gently pierced with a fork, and the flesh should not appear translucent in the middle (except for salmon and tuna). Take into account the fact that fish will continue to cook a little after you have removed it from the heat source.

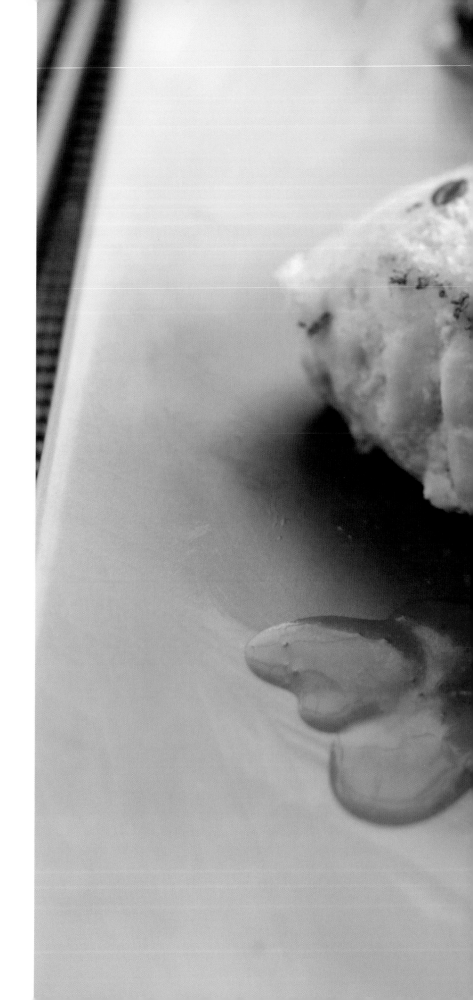

fish

butterfish

(Peprilus simillimus)

general description

No self-respecting traditional Hawaiian luau would be complete without butterfish, typically served *laulau:* wrapped in green taro leaves and steamed. Hawaiian butterfish is a type of pomfret that is closely related to the Atlantic butterfish (*Peprilus triacanthus*), which was salted and brought to the islands by the early New England whaling crews. Pacific butterfish (also called oilfish) is small—typically 6 to 8 inches in length and up to a pound in weight—thin, and silvery, with a strikingly forked tail.

uses, flavor, and cooking qualities

Butterfish is usually served whole, and if you see "butterfish fillets," they are probably sablefish, also called black cod (which is not a cod at all, but a skilfish), or walu (*Ruvettus pretiosus*), a type of mackerel popular in Fiji and other South Pacific islands, also known as oilfish or escolar. At Roy's, the term *butterfish* refers to a style of presentation rather than a specific species of fish. For this purpose, we typically use sablefish or black cod fillets and marinate them with miso to give the fish a rich, buttery texture. In the case of true butterfish, the high fat content gives it a rich mouth feel when cooked. The flaky, tender white flesh of Pacific butterfish has a mild but tasty flavor and tends to be bony. Butterfish is usually sautéed or grilled whole.

substitutions

Atlantic butterfish, walu (see above), sablefish (black cod), halibut, and pompano.

butterfish recipes

Pan-Seared Butterfish with Coconut–Luau Leaf Sauce and Kalua Pork Miso | 10

Miso-Crusted Butterfish with Lemon-Parsley Sauce and Sweet Soy Drizzle | 13

pan-seared butterfish with coconut– luau leaf sauce and kalua pork miso

Serves 4 as a main course

If you have ever been to a traditional Hawaiian luau, then you have probably eaten butterfish and luau leaf (the leaf of the wetland taro plant). This dish is my modern twist on classic luau ingredients. In this recipe, you could omit the pork, but it does complement the fish beautifully, and it really makes a great combination with the sauce. The luau-style tomato side dish rounds it all out perfectly. See page 236 for the availability of frozen luau leaves.

Kalua Pork Miso

- 3 pounds pork butt (pork shoulder)
- 8 cups chicken stock (page 219)
- 2 tablespoons liquid smoke, or to taste
- Salt and freshly ground black pepper

Miso Glaze

- ½ cup mirin
- ⅓ cup white miso (shiro miso)
- ¼ cup maple syrup
- 3 tablespoons sugar

Coconut–Luau Leaf Sauce

- 1 tablespoon sesame oil
- 1 teaspoon minced garlic
- 1 teaspoon minced fresh ginger
- 2 cups reserved pork stock, above
- ½ cup frozen luau leaves, thawed
- ½ cup demi-glace (page 221)
- ¼ cup canned coconut milk
- ½ cup packed chopped spinach leaves

Butterfish

- 2 tablespoons sesame oil
- 4 (6-ounce) butterfish or sablefish (black cod) fillets
- Salt

Lomi lomi tomatoes (page 225)
Fresh chives, for garnish

Preheat the oven to 350°F. To prepare the pork, roll the pork butt into a cylinder about 3 inches in diameter and tie at intervals with kitchen twine. Put the stock in a saucepan, add the liquid smoke, and bring to a simmer. Add the pork, season with salt and pepper, cover the pan with aluminum foil, and transfer to the oven. Braise for about 1 hour or until tender. (Alternatively, the pork can be cooked over low heat on the stove top.) Transfer the pork to a plate and recover with the foil. Set aside and keep warm. Reserve the stock.

To prepare the glaze, combine the mirin, miso, and maple syrup in a saucepan. Whisk in the sugar. Cook over medium heat for about 10 minutes, or until the mixture is syrupy. Remove from the heat and set aside.

continued

continued
from page 10

To prepare the sauce, heat the sesame oil in a heavy saucepan over medium-high heat. Add the garlic and ginger and sauté for 30 seconds. Add the reserved kalua pork stock and the luau leaves. Cook to reduce the liquid by half. Add the demi-glace and coconut milk and cook to reduce until the sauce coats the back of a spoon, 8 to 10 minutes. Transfer the sauce to a blender, add the spinach, and purée. Strain the sauce into a clean saucepan. Set aside and keep warm.

Preheat the broiler.

To prepare the fish, heat the oil in a heavy nonstick sauté pan or skillet over medium-high heat. Season the butterfish with salt to taste, add to the pan, and sauté for about 3 minutes on each side, or until opaque throughout.

While the fish is cooking, slice the warm pork and transfer to a shallow baking dish or roasting pan. Pour 1/4 cup of the glaze over the pork. Place under the broiler 5 to 6 inches from the heat source and broil for 2 minutes, until the glaze is golden brown. Place a quarter of the pork on a small warmed plate. Top with the lomi lomi tomatoes and garnish with the chives. Place the sauce in the center of a separate plate and arrange the butterfish on top.

(Alternatively, arrange each serving of pork and butterfish together on a warmed plate, with the fish on top of pork. Spoon the warm sauce around and top the fish with the lomi lomi tomatoes.)

miso-crusted butterfish with lemon-parsley sauce and sweet soy drizzle

Serves 4 as a main course

Marinating fish in miso is a traditional Japanese preparation, and I owe the idea for this recipe to Nobu Matsuhisa, one of the great ambassadors of Japanese cuisine. Nobu used the technique while starring as a guest chef at one of our recent anniversary dinners at Roy's in Honolulu, and I have transformed his dish into a Hawaiian Fusion style. The miso forms a subtle caramelized crust that can also be used with other fish, especially sea bass and grouper. Note that ideally the fish should marinate overnight.

Miso Marinade and Butterfish

1 cup sugar

1 1/4 cups white miso (shiro miso)

1/2 cup sake

1/2 cup mirin

4 (6-ounce) butterfish or sablefish (black cod) fillets

Lemon-Parsley Sauce

Juice of 1 lemon

1 cup warm beurre blanc (page 223)

Sweet Soy Drizzle

1 cup soy sauce

1 cup sugar

Steamed rice (page 227), for serving

To prepare the marinade and fish, combine the sugar, miso, sake, and mirin in a saucepan and whisk to blend. Bring to a boil over high heat, then decrease the heat to low and simmer for 45 minutes, stirring occasionally. Remove from the heat, transfer to a shallow dish, and let cool completely. Add the butterfish and refrigerate overnight.

To prepare the sauce, stir the lemon juice into the beurre blanc. Set aside and keep warm over tepid water. To prepare the soy drizzle, combine the soy sauce and sugar in a small saucepan. Stir over low heat until the sugar dissolves. Continue to cook for about 15 minutes, or until reduced to 1 cup.

Heat a dry heavy stainless-steel sauté pan or skillet over medium heat for 2 to 3 minutes. Remove the fish from the marinade and sear for 3 to 4 minutes on each side, until opaque throughout. Transfer to warmed plates and pour the sauce around the fish. Spoon the soy drizzle over the sauce and serve with the rice alongside the butterfish.

ehu

short-tailed red snapper

(Etelis carbunculus)

general description

Ehu is also known as the squirrelfish snapper or yellow-striped red snapper due to the thin lateral yellow stripe along its bright red body (for notes on snapper, see pages 61, 85, and 143). Like its close cousin the onaga, ehu prefers the habitat of deep reefs, 600 to 1,000 feet below the surface. At fish markets, ehu typically weigh from 1 pound to over 10 pounds and can measure up to 2 feet in length; they are mostly caught by hook and line. As with onaga, in some markets (especially on the West Coast), red rockfish is also marketed as Pacific red snapper. There are several types of rockfish, and while some are similar in flavor and texture to ehu and onaga, others are noticeably inferior. As true snapper is expensive, try to verify your purchase.

uses, flavor, and cooking qualities

Peak season for ehu is during the winter. It has white to pale pink flesh that turns white when cooked. Its texture is soft, and its flavor is a little less refined and delicate than that of onaga or opakapaka. Ehu is a versatile fish that can be prepared in similar ways to other snappers.

substitutions

Other snappers, particularly onaga (long-tailed red snapper), gray snapper (uku), and Atlantic red snapper, as well as sea bass or grouper.

ehu recipes

Lemongrass-and-Cilantro-Crusted Ehu with Sweet
   Black Rice and Mango | 17

Mediterranean-Style Ehu with Penne Pasta, Anchovies,
   and Tomatoes | 18

lemongrass-and-cilantro-crusted ehu with sweet black rice and mango

Serves 4 as a main course

Thai black rice, available at specialty stores and well-stocked Asian markets, makes a striking color contrast with any white-fleshed fish and many other foods. Like wild rice (which is not related, but which can be substituted here), black rice has a pleasantly crunchy texture and a nutty flavor. You can, if you wish, use basmati or jasmine rice instead of black rice, and you can substitute onaga or opakapaka for the ehu, if you like.

Sweet Black Rice and Mango

1½ cups water

1 cup Thai black rice

¾ cup canned coconut milk

½ cup diced mango

Salt and freshly ground black pepper

Lemongrass and Cilantro Crust

4 teaspoons minced fresh lemongrass

4 teaspoons finely sliced scallion (green parts only)

2 tablespoons fresh cilantro leaves

Freshly cracked black pepper

½ cup fish sauce

¼ cup soy sauce

½ cup canola oil

4 (6-ounce) ehu fillets

1 red bell pepper, seeded, deribbed, and julienned, for garnish (optional)

To prepare the rice, bring the water to a boil in a saucepan and add the rice. Simmer for about 15 minutes, or until tender. Drain the rice and transfer to a bowl.

While the rice is cooking, pour the coconut milk into a saucepan and bring to a boil. Cook until reduced by half; it will be thick and creamy in consistency. Stir in the cooked rice and the mango. Season with salt and pepper to taste. Set aside and keep warm.

To prepare the crust, combine the lemongrass, scallion, cilantro, and pepper to taste. Pour the fish sauce and soy sauce into a shallow baking dish and stir to mix. Crust the ehu on one side with the crust mixture and transfer to the baking dish, crust side up. Let stand for 5 minutes. Heat the canola oil in a large nonstick sauté pan or skillet over medium-high heat. Sauté the fish for 2 to 3 minutes on each side, or until opaque throughout. Transfer to warmed plates and serve with the rice alongside. Garnish with the julienned red pepper.

mediterranean-style ehu with penne pasta, anchovies, and tomatoes

Serves 4 as a main course

This is the kind of dish I enjoy eating after a hard day's work in the restaurant. It's a bit spicy, and the combination of Mediterranean ingredients—anchovies, tomatoes, pancetta, and penne pasta—gives the finished plate a rich and comforting feel. You can use any type of snapper, and surprisingly, lamb also matches up well with these ingredients. To accentuate the style of the dish even more, sprinkle a little feta cheese over the top.

Marinade and Fish

1 cup dry white wine

¼ cup olive oil

1 cup sliced Maui or other sweet white onion

3 cloves garlic, minced

¼ cup coarsely chopped fresh basil

Leaves from 3 sprigs thyme, minced

4 (6-ounce) ehu fillets

Penne Pasta

1½ pounds penne pasta

3 tomatoes, peeled and seeded (see page 228)

¼ cup olive oil

3 cloves garlic, finely sliced

¼ cup diced pancetta

3 anchovy fillets, minced

2 teaspoons minced red Thai chile

2 shallots, finely sliced

1 cup packed coarsely chopped spinach

Salt and freshly ground black pepper

Prepare a medium-hot fire in a charcoal grill or preheat a gas grill to 450°F.

To prepare the marinade, combine the wine and oil in a shallow baking dish and stir in the onion, garlic, basil, and thyme. Add the ehu and marinate for 15 minutes on each side.

Meanwhile, cook the penne in a large pot of salted boiling water until al dente, 8 to 10 minutes. Drain and set aside. Purée the tomatoes in a blender or food processor. Set aside.

Heat the olive oil in a large sauté pan or skillet over medium-high heat. Add the garlic, pancetta, anchovies, chile, and shallots and sauté for about 1 minute, or until fragrant. Add the spinach, puréed tomatoes, and cooked pasta. Increase the heat to high and sauté for about 2 minutes, or until heated through. Season with salt and pepper to taste.

Remove the ehu from the marinade and grill for 2 to 3 minutes on each side, or until opaque throughout. To serve, divide the pasta among warmed pasta bowls and top each serving with a grilled ehu fillet.

hawaiian sea bass

hapu'upu'u or grouper

(Epinepheus quernus)

general description

The Hawaiian sea bass is in fact a type of grouper (Seale's grouper), which in turn
is a subgroup of the sea bass family, so it is related to the more familiar black bass
and striped bass (sea bass is the largest family of fish in the world). Groupers are
often found near coral reefs and rocky outcroppings as well as in the open ocean,
and they are usually caught with hook and line. The Hawaiian sea bass grows
slowly—typically, up to 3 feet in length—and the females have the unusual her-
maphroditic characteristic of changing into males as they get older. The skin of the
Hawaiian sea bass is dark brown with some white spots, although it can change to
black or dark red to match its surroundings. This fish is most abundant in markets
during the fall and late winter months. It ranges in weight from 5 to 30 pounds and
is usually sold whole, although larger fish are sometimes sold in fillet form.

uses, flavor, and cooking qualities

Like other types of sea bass and grouper, the Hawaiian sea bass is a versatile fish
when it comes to cooking: it can be steamed whole (if small), poached, broiled,
baked, sautéed, or grilled. Hawaiian sea bass has a moist, lean, bright white flesh
that gives it a firm, meaty texture. It has a mild and elegant, slightly sweet flavor
reminiscent of the richness of shellfish.

substitutions

Snappers; other types of sea bass, including striped bass and black bass; grouper,
halibut, mahimahi, and tilefish.

sea bass / grouper recipes

seared sea bass with wok-sautéed rice noodles, pork, and shrimp

Serves 4 as a main course

Stir-fried noodles make a tasty bed for fish dishes, and the particular inspiration for this recipe comes from Thai-style rice noodles, which are a favorite of mine whenever I eat out at Thai restaurants. As the butterfish recipe on page 10 proves, pork adds another flavor and texture dimension to fish and seafood dishes, and the shrimp serves the same purpose. Use palm sugar for this recipe if you can, as the flavor is superior to that of refined sugar.

Rice Noodles, Pork, and Shrimp

- 3 tablespoons soy sauce
- 3 tablespoons fish sauce
- 2 tablespoons palm sugar
- ½ cup thinly sliced pork belly or pork butt (pork shoulder)
- ¼ cup sesame oil
- 2 teaspoons minced garlic
- 2 red Thai chiles, seeded and minced
- 1 shallot, minced
- 8 ounces extra-large shrimp (about 8), peeled, deveined, and halved lengthwise
- 1 pound white rice noodles

Rice Noodles, Pork, and Shrimp, continued

- 1 cup bean sprouts
- 4 baby bok choy, quartered
- 2 tomatoes, quartered
- ¼ cup packed fresh mint leaves

Sea Bass

- 2 tablespoons sesame oil
- 4 sea bass fillets, about 7 ounces each
- Salt and freshly ground black pepper

Combine the soy sauce, fish sauce, and palm sugar in a bowl and stir until the palm sugar dissolves. Set aside.

Heat a wok over high heat and add the pork. Cook for 2 to 3 minutes, until some of the pork fat is rendered. Add the oil, and when hot, add the garlic, chiles, and shallot. Stir-fry for about 1 minute, until the garlic begins to brown, and then add the shrimp. Cook until the shrimp begin to curl slightly, about 1 minute; do not overcook or the shrimp will become tough. Add the rice noodles, bean sprouts, bok choy, tomatoes, and mint leaves and stir-fry about 1 minute longer. Pour in the soy sauce mixture and stir to deglaze the wok. Set aside and keep warm.

While cooking the noodles, prepare the fish. Heat the sesame oil in a sauté pan or skillet over medium-high heat. Season the fillets with salt and pepper to taste and add to the pan. Sauté for about 3 minutes on each side, or until opaque throughout. Transfer to warmed plates and serve the rice noodle mixture on the side.

butter-seared sea bass with sweet crab and korean hot pepper sauce

Serves 4 as a main course

When we opened Roy's in New York City's financial district, chef Troy Guard created this dish for our first menu. The crab "bed" for the bass is a preparation we have long served with other types of fish, and the vinaigrette-style sauce was inspired by a potsticker recipe from Roy's in Honolulu. Here, Troy has put together different classic elements from our repertoire in a unique way. Serve this dish with steamed rice, if you like.

Korean Hot Pepper Sauce

¼ cup chopped Maui or other sweet white onion

2 tablespoons chopped daikon

2 tablespoons water

½ tablespoon ko chu jang (Korean chile paste), sambal sekera, or other garlic chile paste

½ cup soy sauce

½ teaspoon minced garlic

½ teaspoon minced fresh ginger

¼ cup rice wine vinegar

1 tablespoon sesame oil

2 teaspoons minced fresh cilantro

1½ teaspoons minced scallions (green parts only)

1 teaspoon white sesame seeds, toasted (page 228)

1 teaspoon black sesame seeds, toasted (page 228)

Sweet Crab Mixture

1 cup dry white wine

1 shallot, minced

2 cups heavy cream

8 ounces fresh lump crabmeat, picked over for shell

2 tablespoons minced fresh basil

4 tablespoons unsalted butter

Salt and freshly ground black pepper

Sea Bass

6 tablespoons unsalted butter

4 sea bass fillets, about 6 ounces each

Salt and freshly ground black pepper

To prepare the hot pepper sauce, combine the onion, daikon, and water in a blender and purée until smooth. Add the chile paste, soy sauce, garlic, and ginger and purée again. Transfer to a bowl and stir in the vinegar, sesame oil, cilantro, scallions, and black and white sesame seeds. Set aside.

To prepare the crab mixture, combine the wine and shallot in a heavy saucepan. Bring to a simmer over medium-high heat and cook to reduce the liquid until almost dry. Add the cream and cook to reduce to about 1/4 cup. Stir in the crabmeat, basil, butter, and salt and pepper to taste. Set aside and keep warm.

To prepare the fish, melt the butter in a heavy stainless-steel sauté pan or skillet over medium-high heat. Season the sea bass with salt and pepper to taste and add to the pan. Sauté for 3 to 4 minutes on each side, until opaque throughout.

To serve, place the crab mixture in the center of each warmed plate. Carefully place the sea bass on top and spoon the hot pepper sauce around the fish.

hawaiian sea bass   25

steamed sea bass with shiitakes, asparagus, and spaetzle in thai curry sauce

Serves 4 as a main course

Spaetzle is a comfort food that I always enjoy, and although it's usually paired with red meat, it provided the starting point for this dish. The result is a hearty fusion dish combining a Thai curry sauce, Pacific Rim flavors, and European spaetzle. Grouper or mahimahi works equally well in this recipe.

Spaetzle

3 large eggs

1½ cups milk

1¾ cups all-purpose flour

1 teaspoon salt

2 tablespoons olive oil

Thai Curry Sauce

¼ cup canola oil

2 teaspoons minced garlic

1 teaspoon minced fresh ginger

1 tablespoon sliced lemongrass (white part only)

1 cup canned coconut milk

2 tablespoons fish sauce

1 tablespoon palm sugar or firmly packed dark brown sugar

2 tablespoons Thai yellow curry paste

4 fresh mint leaves

10 fresh basil leaves, preferably Thai basil

Sea Bass

8 shiitake mushrooms, stemmed (reserve stems)

Stems from 1 bunch fresh cilantro

1 piece unpeeled ginger, about 2 inches long

2 lemongrass stalks (white part only), peeled

4 sea bass fillets, about 6 ounces each

Salt and freshly ground black pepper

½ cup olive oil

4 ounces pancetta, finely diced

8 garlic cloves, minced

12 asparagus spears, trimmed and cut into 1-inch diagonal lengths

1 artichoke bottom, cooked and julienned

1 bunch spinach, steamed and washed

Salt and freshly ground black pepper

Fresh basil, for garnish (optional)

To prepare the spaetzle, whisk the eggs and milk together in a bowl. Add the flour and salt and whisk well; the batter should be thick. Bring a large saucepan of water to a boil and prepare an ice bath in a large bowl. Using a wooden spoon, push the batter through a colander into the boiling water and cook until the dumplings rise to the top, about 1 minute. Remove the dumplings with a slotted spoon and transfer to the ice bath to stop the cooking process. When cool, drain the dumplings and pat dry. Transfer to a bowl, toss with the olive oil, and set aside.

continued

continued
from page 26

To prepare the sauce, heat the oil in a heavy saucepan over medium-high heat. Stir in the garlic, ginger, and sliced lemongrass, then the coconut milk, fish sauce, palm sugar, curry paste, mint, and basil. Cook, stirring, for 2 to 3 minutes, until thoroughly combined. Remove from the heat and set aside.

To prepare the fish, add 1 to 2 inches water to a steamer. Place the shiitake stems, cilantro stems, ginger, and lemongrass on a rimmed dish that can fit inside a steamer, and bring the water to a boil. Season the fish with salt and pepper to taste and add to the rimmed plate. Cover and steam for about 8 minutes, or until the fish is opaque throughout.

While the fish is cooking, heat ¼ cup of the olive oil in a large, heavy skillet or sauté pan over medium heat. Add the pancetta and sauté for about 3 minutes, or until golden brown. Using a slotted spoon, transfer the pancetta to paper towels to drain. Increase the heat to high until the oil in the pan is hot and shimmering, then add the remaining ¼ cup oil. Add the spaetzle and sauté for about 2 minutes until golden brown. Add the garlic, asparagus, shiitake caps, and artichoke, and sauté 2 minutes longer, until the mushrooms are tender and the asparagus is crisp tender. Add the spinach, toss with the other ingredients, and sauté for about 1 minute, or until lightly wilted.

Season the spaetzle and vegetable mixture with salt and pepper to taste and transfer to the center of warmed plates. Remove the fish from the steamer, arrange on top of the vegetables, and spoon the warm sauce around the fish. Place the fresh basil leaves on top to serve.

jade pesto–steamed sea bass with filipino sizzling soy vinaigrette

Serves 4 as a main course

The credit for this dish belongs to Gordon Hopkins, director of chefs for Roy's restaurants and a business partner since the first day we opened. Gordon created it especially for a wine dinner we held at Roy's in Honolulu. The flavors of the pesto and the vinaigrette are complementary as well as assertive, so coat the fish lightly with the pesto so as not to overwhelm it. The pesto can be stored in an airtight container in the refrigerator for up to 2 days. Serve this dish with your favorite vegetable.

Jade Pesto

1 tablespoon peanut oil

1½ tablespoons oyster sauce

1½ teaspoons water

¼ cup coarsely chopped scallions (green parts only)

¼ cup fresh cilantro leaves

¾ teaspoon minced fresh ginger

¾ teaspoon minced garlic

Salt and freshly ground black pepper

Soy Vinaigrette

3 tablespoons minced red bell pepper

2 tablespoons minced yellow bell pepper

2 tablespoons minced green bell pepper

2 tablespoons minced scallions (green parts only)

Soy Vinaigrette, continued

2 tablespoons minced fresh cilantro

2 tablespoons grated and minced daikon

2 tablespoons grated and minced Maui or other sweet white onion

½ tablespoon grated and minced fresh ginger

¼ cup peanut oil

2½ tablespoons rice wine vinegar

7 tablespoons soy sauce

1 tablespoon freshly squeezed lemon juice

¼ cup water

Salt and freshly ground black pepper

4 (7-ounce) sea bass fillets

Steamed rice (page 227), for serving

To prepare the pesto, combine the peanut oil, oyster sauce, and water in a blender. Add the scallions, cilantro, ginger, and garlic and purée until smooth. Season with salt and pepper to taste. Cover and set aside.

To prepare the vinaigrette, combine the bell peppers, scallions, cilantro, daikon, onion, and ginger in a metal bowl. Heat the peanut oil in a small saucepan over high heat until just smoking. Carefully pour the hot oil over the vegetables so that they sizzle. Toss to coat evenly. Add the vinegar, soy sauce, lemon juice, and 1/4 cup of water. Season with salt and pepper to taste and set aside.

continued

continued
from page 29 Coat one side of each sea bass fillet with the pesto and transfer to a rimmed dish that can fit inside a steamer. Bring 1 to 2 inches of water to a boil in the steamer and add the bass (cook in two batches if necessary). Steam for 4 to 5 minutes, until opaque throughout. Transfer to warmed plates and arrange on top of the steamed rice. Ladle the vinaigrette around each serving.

garlic-and-sesame-crusted grouper with maui onion–miso vinaigrette

Serves 4 as a main course

This flavorful vinaigrette was created by Steve Potasky when he worked at Roy's at Pebble Beach, and several of our restaurants use it to great effect with fish dishes. Its flavors emerge to their fullest a few hours after it has been prepared, so plan on making it in advance. I think Steve's vinaigrette works best of all with this grouper preparation; you can also use sea bass for equally outstanding results. If you prefer, you can serve this dish with steamed rice instead of (or in addition to) the salad greens.

Maui Onion–Miso Vinaigrette

¼ Maui onion, chopped

3 tablespoons white miso (shiro miso)

2 tablespoons diced daikon

½ bunch scallions (green parts only), chopped

2 tablespoons soy sauce

2 tablespoons sesame oil

2 tablespoons peanut oil

2 tablespoons ginger juice (page 231)

2 tablespoons rice wine vinegar

1 tablespoon furikake

1 tablespoon Soy Mustard Sauce (page 121, optional)

1 teaspoon wasabi powder

1 teaspoon shichimi

1 tablespoon white sesame seeds, toasted (page 228)

1 tablespoon black sesame seeds, toasted (page 228)

Salad Greens

½ cup arugula

½ cup frisée lettuce

½ cup radicchio

Crust and Fish

½ cup panko (Japanese bread crumbs)

¼ cup minced garlic

2 tablespoons white sesame seeds, toasted (page 228)

2 tablespoons black sesame seeds, toasted (page 228)

4 (6-ounce) grouper fillets

Salt and freshly ground black pepper

2 tablespoons peanut oil

To prepare the vinaigrette, combine the onion, miso, daikon, and scallions in a blender and add the soy sauce, sesame oil, peanut oil, ginger juice, vinegar, furikake, soy mustard, wasabi, and shichimi. Blend until emulsified. Transfer to a bowl or airtight container and whisk in the black and white sesame seeds. Cover and refrigerate for at least 3 to 4 hours or overnight.

Toss the salad greens together in a bowl and set aside.

To prepare the crust, combine the panko, garlic, and black and white sesame seeds in a bowl and stir to combine thoroughly. Season the fish with salt and pepper to taste and dredge on one side in the panko mixture. Heat the peanut oil in a heavy stainless-steel sauté pan or skillet over medium-high heat. Add the fish, crust side down, and sear for about 3 minutes or until the crust is golden brown. Turn over and sauté for about 3 minutes longer, or until opaque throughout. Transfer the fish to warmed plates, crust side up, and ladle some of the vinaigrette around the fish. Garnish with the salad greens, drizzling them with some of the vinaigrette.

mahimahi
dorado or dolphin fish
(Coryphaena hippurus)

general description

Relax—this fish is unrelated to Flipper, the lovable mammal. Mahimahi, found in warm open-ocean waters around the world, is one of the most colorful fish in the water, with a greenish-blue and silvery skin dappled with yellow on its sides and belly, and tinted with iridescent blue, gold, and bright green markings—but it fades to a dull gray once landed. Mahimahi has a distinctive profile, with a blunt, heavy-looking forehead (in male fish), a tapering body, and a large, forked tail. It is caught year-round, but it tends to be more abundant in the late spring and during the fall. Most mahimahi is caught by trollers and is landed between 10 and 35 pounds, with some over 50 pounds. It is a very fast and acrobatic swimmer, sometimes leaping out of the water.

uses, flavor, and cooking qualities

Mahimahi is sold both in fillet and steak form. It has thin skin, with a firm but slightly flaky white to light pink flesh that turns off-white when cooked. It has a medium fat content and a succulent, delicate, slightly sweet flavor. Some people describe the flavor of mahimahi as "gamier" than that of opakapaka and other snappers, and I think they mean that it has more dimensions of flavor. It's certainly a favorite fish in Hawaii. It takes well to marinades, and its firm texture lends itself to grilling, sautéing, steaming, or broiling.

substitutions

Other firm-fleshed white fish, such as grouper, sea bass, snapper, swordfish, halibut, tilefish, and ono.

mahimahi recipes

garlic-and-peppercorn-crusted mahimahi with sherry–blue cheese cream sauce

Serves 4 as a main course

Sometimes, as the saying goes, necessity is the mother of invention. Well, this is an off-the-wall dish that I created late one night at Roy's out of necessity. I'd run out of recipes and the usual ingredients for preparing mahimahi, so I decided to try some unusual combinations of ingredients. Fortunately, everything came together nicely, and this is a recipe that has often been reprised at my restaurants. My preference is to serve this dish with sautéed spinach.

Sherry–Blue Cheese Cream Sauce

2 tablespoons olive oil

1 tablespoon minced shallot

1 teaspoon minced garlic

2 tablespoons sherry vinegar

¼ cup chicken stock (page 219)

1 tablespoon minced fresh basil

½ cup demi-glace (page 221)

2 tablespoons crumbled blue cheese

½ cup heavy cream

Salt and freshly ground black pepper

Mahimahi

1 tablespoon minced garlic

1 tablespoon minced shallot

Salt to taste, preferably Hawaiian white or red salt

1 tablespoon freshly cracked black pepper

4 (7-ounce) mahimahi fillets

To prepare the sauce, heat the oil in a heavy saucepan over medium-high heat. Add the shallot and garlic and sauté for 1 minute. Add the vinegar and stir. Immediately add the chicken stock, basil, and demi-glace and bring to a simmer. Stir in the blue cheese and cream and decrease the heat to medium. Cook to reduce the mixture for 5 minutes, or until the sauce is thick enough to coat the back of a spoon. Season with salt and pepper to taste. Set aside and keep warm.

To prepare the mahimahi, mix together the garlic, shallot, salt, and pepper in a bowl. Crust one side of each fillet with the mixture. Heat a dry stainless-steel sauté pan or skillet over medium-high heat for 2 to 3 minutes. Sear the mahimahi for 2 to 3 minutes on each side, or until opaque throughout.

To serve, ladle the sauce onto warmed plates and arrange the mahimahi on top of the sauce.

macadamia nut—crusted mahimahi with thai-style coconut-basil sauce

Serves 4 as a main course

One of the major food events to take place in Hawaii over recent years has been the annual Cuisines of the Sun gathering at the Mauna Lani Bay Hotel and Resort on the Kona coast of the Big Island. It has always been a fun event, and I have found myself learning something new each time. A few years back, a Thai chef made a guest appearance and served the best coconut curry I had ever tasted. It inspired me to use coconut milk more often and to make this sauce combining salty dried shrimp and fish sauce, sweet palm sugar and coconut milk, and fragrant basil. Dried shrimp are available at Asian stores and markets. Serve this dish with sticky rice and your favorite vegetable.

Coconut-Basil Sauce

2 tablespoons olive oil

1 tablespoon minced fresh ginger

1 tablespoon minced garlic

1 teaspoon minced dried shrimp

2 teaspoons fish sauce

1 cup chicken stock (page 219)

1 cup canned coconut milk

1 tablespoon palm sugar

10 fresh basil leaves, finely shredded

Crust and Mahimahi

4 (7-ounce) mahimahi fillets

Salt and freshly ground black pepper

2 tablespoons crushed macadamia nuts

To prepare the sauce, heat the oil in a heavy sauté pan or skillet over medium-high heat. Add the ginger, garlic, and dried shrimp and sauté for 2 minutes. Add the fish sauce and stir to deglaze the pan. Immediately add the chicken stock, coconut milk, palm sugar, and basil and bring to a simmer. Continue to simmer for 2 or 3 minutes, until the sauce is thick enough to coat the back of a spoon. Set aside and keep warm.

To prepare the crust and fish, season the fillets with salt and pepper to taste on each side. Spread the macadamia nuts on a plate and crust the mahimahi fillet on one side only with the nuts. Heat a stainless-steel sauté pan or skillet over medium-high heat for 2 to 3 minutes. Sear the mahimahi for 2 to 3 minutes on each side, or until opaque throughout. Transfer to warmed plates and spoon the sauce around the fish.

steamed mahimahi with chinese-style black bean sauce

Serves 4 as a main course

The firm, rich texture and mild flavor of mahimahi take well to steaming, and for the same reasons, you can substitute cod in this recipe, or even salmon. Here, a Chinese-style black bean sauce complements fish cooked in a traditional Chinese method. I like to serve this dish with jasmine rice and stir-fried vegetables.

Mahimahi and Sauce

1 tablespoon cornstarch

2 tablespoons water

¼ cup soy sauce

¼ cup brandy

2½ tablespoons sugar

4 (7-ounce) mahimahi fillets

2 tablespoons minced pork fat or bacon fat

2 tablespoons coarsely minced fermented black beans

2 tablespoons minced fresh ginger

1 tablespoon minced garlic

3 scallions (green parts only), cut into 2-inch julienne

8 dried shiitake mushrooms, soaked in water overnight, sliced

Garnish

¼ cup daikon sprouts

1 teaspoon white sesame seeds, toasted (page 228)

2 tablespoons finely sliced scallions (green parts only)

1 teaspoon rayu (spicy sesame oil)

In a bowl, mix together the cornstarch and water to make a paste. Stir in the soy sauce, brandy, and sugar. Set aside.

In a saucepan of boiling water, blanch the mahimahi for about 30 seconds. Using a slotted spoon, transfer to a rimmed plate that can be used for steaming. Bring 1 inch of water in the bottom of a steamer to a boil.

Meanwhile, in a heavy saucepan, render the pork fat over medium-high heat. Add the black beans, ginger, and garlic and sauté for about 1 minute. Add half of the julienned scallions and all the shiitakes and sauté 30 seconds longer. Add the cornstarch mixture and stir until the sauce thickens. Carefully pour over the fish on the plate and sprinkle with the remaining scallions. Carefully place the plate in the steamer, cover, and steam for 4 to 5 minutes, until opaque throughout.

continued

continued from page 37 To prepare the garnish, combine the sprouts, sesame seeds, sliced scallions, and rayu in a bowl and toss to mix. To serve, carefully transfer the fish from the steamer to warmed plates. Spoon some of the sauce over the fish and sprinkle the garnish on top.

grilled mahimahi with bamboo, edamame, and turmeric rice in a tamarind curry sauce

Serves 4 as a main course

recipe pictured on page 40 One of my favorite foods, especially when I travel to Japan, is curried rice. It's a late-night comfort food for me that's just perfect with a glass of beer. It surprises a lot of people to learn that curry is a typical feature of Japanese home cooking that has long been very popular; it's something that I grew up with. This fusion dish combines these roots with Asian ingredients—I enjoy the Indian flavors of coriander, turmeric, and tamarind, although I use them all too rarely.

Tamarind Curry Sauce

- 1½ tablespoons tamarind pulp
- ¼ cup warm water
- 1 tablespoon canola oil
- 1 tablespoon minced garlic
- 1 tablespoon minced fresh ginger
- 1 stalk lemongrass (white part only), peeled and thinly sliced
- 2 fresh or frozen kaffir lime leaves, thinly sliced
- 2 shallots, minced
- 2 tablespoons dried shrimp
- 2 teaspoons curry powder
- 1 teaspoon coriander seeds
- ¼ teaspoon ground turmeric
- 1 Roma tomato, chopped
- 1 can (19 ounces) coconut milk

Turmeric Rice

- 2 tablespoons canola oil
- ½ tablespoon minced garlic
- 1 teaspoon minced fresh ginger
- 1 stalk lemongrass (white part only), peeled and sliced into 1-inch lengths
- 2 teaspoons ground turmeric
- 1½ cups long-grain rice
- 1½ cups chicken stock (page 219)
- 2 tablespoons fish sauce
- 1 ½ tablespoons palm sugar
- ¼ cup minced fresh cilantro

Vegetables

2 tablespoons canola oil

1 teaspoon minced garlic

1 teaspoon minced fresh ginger

1 (8-ounce) can sliced bamboo shoots, drained

1 cup edamame or frozen peas

15 shiitake mushroom caps, sliced

4 ounces haricots verts or baby Blue Lake green beans, trimmed

Salt and freshly ground black pepper

3 tablespoons oyster sauce

4 mahimahi fillets, about 6 ounces each

Salt and freshly ground black pepper to taste

Prepare a grill.

To prepare the sauce, put the tamarind in a bowl, add the water, and let stand for about 10 minutes. Meanwhile, heat the oil in a heavy saucepan over medium-high heat. Add the garlic, ginger, lemongrass, lime leaves, shallots, and dried shrimp and sauté for 1 minute. Add the curry powder, coriander seeds, and turmeric, stir well, and sauté 1 minute longer. Add the rehydrated tamarind to the saucepan along with the tomato and coconut milk. Bring to a simmer, decrease the heat to low, and simmer for 15 to 20 minutes, until the sauce coats the back of a spoon. Strain into a clean saucepan.

To prepare the rice, heat the oil in a heavy saucepan over medium-high heat. Add the garlic, ginger, lemongrass, and turmeric and sauté for 1 minute. Stir in the rice, then the chicken stock, cover the pan, and cook for about 15 minutes, or until the rice is tender and the liquid is absorbed. Remove from heat. Stir in the fish sauce, palm sugar, and cilantro.

While the rice is cooking, prepare the vegetables: Heat the oil in a large, heavy sauté pan or skillet over medium-high heat. Add the garlic and ginger and sauté for about 30 seconds. Add the bamboo, edamame, shiitakes, and green beans and season with salt and pepper to taste. Sauté for about 2 minutes, or until crisp-tender. Stir in the oyster sauce and cook for about 30 seconds longer, or until the ingredients are well coated.

Season the mahimahi with salt and pepper to taste and grill for 2 to 3 minutes on each side, until opaque throughout. Transfer to warmed plates and pour the warm sauce around the fish. Serve with the rice and vegetables.

grilled mahimahi with bamboo, edamame,
and tumeric rice in a tamarind curry
sauce (recipe on pages 38–39)

pan-seared mahimahi with eggplant misoyaki

Serves 4 as a main course

This recipe was inspired by childhood memories of my mother cooking eggplant in the Okinawan style, with miso. It was a dish I was particularly fond of, and here I've added my two cents' worth to my mother's recipe and paired it with fish, which makes a great combination. Serve with steamed rice.

Eggplant Misoyaki

- ¼ cup red miso (aka miso)
- 2 tablespoons sugar
- 1 tablespoon mirin
- 1 tablespoon sake
- 4 Japanese eggplants, halved lengthwise
- ¼ cup olive oil

Mahimahi

- 4 (7-ounce) mahimahi fillets
- Salt and freshly ground black pepper
- ¼ cup olive oil

Prepare a medium-hot fire in a charcoal grill or preheat a gas grill to 450°F. Preheat the broiler.

To prepare the eggplant, combine the miso, sugar, mirin, and sake in a bowl. Stir until the sugar dissolves. Score the eggplant halves in a crisscross pattern, about ¹⁄₁₆ inch deep and ½ inch apart, and brush with the olive oil. Grill the eggplant, flesh side down, for 3 to 4 minutes, until cooked halfway through. Transfer to a roasting pan and baste the eggplant skin with the miso mixture. Place under the broiler, flesh side up, and cook 3 to 4 minutes longer, until the eggplant skin is caramelized. Set aside and keep warm.

To prepare the mahimahi, season it with salt and pepper to taste. Heat the oil in a stainless-steel sauté pan or skillet over medium-high heat until the oil is hot and shimmering. Sear the fish for 2 to 3 minutes on each side, until opaque throughout.

To serve, place 2 eggplant halves in parallel fashion on each plate and arrange the fish on top.

marlin

a'u or spearfish

general description

Ancient Hawaiians fished for marlin from outrigger canoes, and today it is caught in significant numbers by longline commercial fishermen in Hawaii. A large part of the commercial catch is shipped to Japan, where marlin is particularly prized for sashimi. Marlin is also a popular open-ocean game fish; the Kona Coast of the Big Island in particular is a center for marlin sportfishing and hosts a prestigious annual Billfish Tournament. Marlin use their spearlike bill to defend themselves and to stun their prey by slashing their bill from side to side. With their long bills, marlin most nearly resemble swordfish (see page 109), but their flesh is leaner and more like that of tuna.

uses, flavor, and cooking qualities

Most marlin is sold in steak form, without the skin, which is tough and inedible. Both blue marlin and striped marlin have a medium-high fat content, a mild flavor, and a tender texture, suiting them for sashimi. The firm, meaty flesh of marlin becomes tender and flaky when cooked. It takes well to grilling and can be successfully smoked. Marlin also freezes well.

substitutions

Marlin recipes can be prepared using other firm-fleshed fish, such as tuna, sword-fish, and mahimahi.

There are several varieties of marlin, but the two most common in Hawaii are:

BLUE MARLIN OR KAJIKI (*MAKAIRA NIGRICANS*)

The largest member of the marlin family, the blue marlin is a warm-water fish that can grow to more than 1,500 pounds, but most are landed between 100 and 300 pounds (all the larger fish are female). Native to the Pacific, Atlantic, and Indian Oceans, blue marlin are most abundant in Hawaiian waters during the summer and fall months. The flesh of blue marlin ranges from orange to red, turning a creamy white when cooked.

STRIPED MARLIN OR NAIRAGI (*TETRAPTURUS AUDAX*)

This warm-water fish is found mostly in the Pacific and Indian Oceans. It typically bears fifteen to twenty white or pale blue vertical stripes, although these fade when the fish is taken from the water. The striped marlin has a thinner bill than the blue marlin, and it tends to be smaller; most are landed between 50 and 100 pounds. They are most abundant in Hawaiian waters in winter and spring, due to their migration patterns. The flesh of striped marlin ranges from pink to orange, turning a creamy white when cooked.

marlin recipes

Carpaccio of Nairagi with Grapefruit and
    Asparagus | 45

Cold-Smoked Marlin Salad with Artichokes and Mango
    Purée | 46

carpaccio of nairagi with grapefruit and asparagus

Serves 4 as an appetizer

This is a refreshing salad that I created specifically for nairagi, an underused Pacific fish. It's a dish that is easy to make, healthful, and with plenty of flavor. If nairagi is unavailable, use thinly sliced fresh snapper instead. For more on yuzu, a Japanese citrus fruit, see the glossary.

Vinaigrette

  3 tablespoons olive oil

  1 tablespoon rice wine vinegar

  1 tablespoon freshly squeezed orange juice

  1 tablespoon freshly squeezed grapefruit juice

  3 tablespoons yuzu juice

  4 teaspoons soy sauce

  Salt and freshly ground black pepper

  8 spears green asparagus, trimmed

  8 spears white asparagus, trimmed

  8 ounces sashimi-grade nairagi, cut into four 2 by 4-inch blocks

  4 cups mixed baby salad greens or mesclun mix

  1 pink or Ruby Red grapefruit, peeled and sectioned

To prepare the vinaigrette, combine the olive oil, vinegar, orange juice, grapefruit juice, yuzu juice, soy sauce, and salt and pepper to taste in a blender and blend until emulsified. Set aside.

Prepare an ice bath in a large bowl. Bring a saucepan of salted water to a boil and blanch the green and white asparagus for 3 to 4 minutes, or until just crisp-tender. Transfer the asparagus to the ice bath to stop the cooking process. When cool, drain and set aside. Finely slice the nairagi and arrange in a fan on each chilled serving plate. Place the asparagus in the middle of the nairagi and arrange the salad greens and grapefruit sections on top. Drizzle the vinaigrette over.

cold-smoked marlin salad with artichokes and mango purée

Serves 4 as an appetizer

Marlin is a great "eating fish," but cooking tends to dry it out; cold-smoking marlin is a great way of avoiding that while infusing its meaty texture with flavor, in the same way that salmon takes to smoking. Smoked marlin has always been a popular preparation in Hawaii, and the idea for this recipe stems from that tradition. The sweet mango sauce complements the smoky flavor of the fish nicely, and the Vietnamese-inspired dressing has just enough kick to really tantalize the taste buds. You can substitute aku (skipjack tuna) for the marlin in this recipe.

Smoked Marlin

8 ounces marlin fillet

¼ cup honey

3 cups sugar

1 cup kosher salt

20 black peppercorns

5 sprigs fresh thyme

2 tablespoons olive oil

Mango Purée

1 mango, peeled, pitted, and chopped

3 tablespoons freshly squeezed lemon juice

Pinch of salt

Freshly ground black pepper

Citrus-Chile Dressing

5 tablespoons extra-virgin olive oil

2 tablespoons minced garlic

2 tablespoons minced shallots

1 tablespoon minced lemongrass (white part only)

6 tablespoons freshly squeezed lime juice

2 tablespoons soy sauce

2 tablespoons fish sauce

2 tablespoons seeded and minced red Thai chile or red serrano

1 tablespoon sugar

2 tablespoons olive oil

8 ounces chanterelle mushrooms or shiitake mushrooms

1 teaspoon minced garlic

1 mango, peeled, pitted, and finely sliced

3 cups mixed baby salad greens or mesclun mix

2 cooked artichoke bottoms, sliced

To prepare the marlin, coat both sides of the fillet with the honey and place in a roasting pan. Combine the sugar, kosher salt, peppercorns, and thyme in a bowl and spread over the coated fish. Loosely cover the marlin with plastic wrap and place a second, smaller roasting pan or skillet on top of the fish; add some cans or other weights to the top pan to weigh down the marlin. Refrigerate for 24 hours.

Prepare the smoker. Soak chunks of aromatic hardwood in water for 20 minutes. Place a pan of water in the bottom of the smoker, and build a fire in the smoker with hardwood lump charcoal or charcoal briquettes and an electric starter. Let the charcoal burn down until it is covered with a uniform whitish-gray ash (20 to 30 minutes). Spread the coals out and add the soaked hardwood chunks. Let burn for 5 minutes. Unwrap the fillet and rinse under cold running water. Rub the fillet with olive oil. Place the fish on the grill over the water pan and cover with the top of the smoker. Smoke for 1 hour.

Alternatively, you can use a wok to smoke the fish. You will need a wok with a matching lid, and 2 wire racks of different heights that will fit inside the wok. Place a handful of wood chips in the bottom of the wok and set a plate of ice cubes on the lower rack. Set the wok over medium heat, and when the wood chips begin to smoke, remove the wok from the heat, and place the fish on the higher rack, above the ice. Immediately cover the wok with the lid and let it absorb the smoke for 5 to 30 minutes.

Meanwhile, prepare the mango purée and the dressing. To prepare the purée, combine the mango, lemon juice, salt, and pepper to taste in a blender and purée until smooth. Cover and refrigerate.

To prepare the dressing, heat the olive oil in a heavy sauté pan or skillet over medium-high heat. Add the garlic, shallots, and lemongrass and sauté for 1 to 2 minutes, until lightly golden brown. Transfer to a mixing bowl and stir in the lime juice, soy sauce, fish sauce, chile, and sugar until combined.

Heat the olive oil in a sauté pan over medium-high heat. Sauté the chanterelles and garlic for 3 to 4 minutes, or until tender.

Arrange the mango slices on chilled serving plates at the 8 o'clock position. In a salad bowl, toss together the salad greens, artichokes, and dressing and arrange on the center of each plate. Finely slice the smoked marlin on a diagonal and place on top of the salad. Sprinkle the mushrooms around the salad and drizzle the mango purée around each plate.

moi

pacific threadfin

(Polydactylus sexfilis)

general description

Moi, related to the sea bream and porgy, was the preferred fish of the *ali'i,* the ancient Hawaiian royalty, who considered it a great delicacy. All other Hawaiians were forbidden to eat "the fish of kings," a transgression punishable by death. The *ali'i* constructed enclosed coastal fishponds to raise moi, an early—and effective—form of fish farming. Moi is still prized, and in Hawaii it is mostly farm-raised in a natural environment as moi is relatively rare in the wild, in Hawaiian waters; commercial fishponds exist on Molokai, windward Oahu, and the Big Island. In addition, at least one Hawaiian aquaculture company—Cates International—raises moi 40 feet below the open ocean surface and 100 feet above the sea floor, using special enclosures that are secured to the seabed. Randy Cates's moi is sold exclusively by Tropic Fish in Honolulu (see page 236).

uses, flavor, and cooking qualities

Moi has tender, moist white to light gray flesh and a delicate, mild flavor. It is usually harvested when it reaches 12 ounces to 1 pound, and sold—and cooked—whole. Moi is highly versatile; it can be steamed, poached, or baked, and it can also be successfully sautéed, grilled, or smoked. It is also used for sashimi. When cooked, the white flesh has a pleasantly flaky yet silky texture, rather like that of butterfish.

substitutions

Snapper and sea bass.

moi recipes

Chinese-Style Steamed Whole Moi with Sizzling Hot
    Peanut Oil | 51

Fresh Fillets of Moi with Peanut Crust and Kula Baby
    Bok Choy | 52

roy's fish and seafood

chinese-style steamed whole moi with sizzling hot peanut oil

Serves 4 as a main course

This Mandarin-style dish is a popular item on our menu, and it's an eye-catching presentation, whether served in our dining room or yours. The dried mushrooms give the dish an earthy, pronounced flavor, but all the senses are engaged by the sizzle, the aromas, and the visual appeal.

4 (12-ounce) whole moi, cleaned

8 dried shiitake mushrooms, soaked overnight in water, drained, and thinly sliced

2 tablespoons very finely julienned ginger

3 scallions (green parts only), very finely julienned

2 leeks (white parts only), cut into 2-inch lengths and julienned

¾ cup soy sauce

2 tablespoons sake

½ cup fish stock or chicken stock (page 219)

2 tablespoons sugar

1 teaspoon salt

½ cup peanut oil

20 cilantro sprigs

Steamed rice (page 227), for serving

In a steamer, bring 1 or 2 inches of water to a boil and add the whole moi. You may have to steam two fish at a time. Cover and steam for 2 minutes. Transfer to a rimmed dish that can fit inside the steamer. Place the shiitakes, ginger, scallions, and leeks on top of the fish. Combine the soy sauce, sake, stock, sugar, and salt in a bowl and stir to blend. Pour over the fish. Place in the steamer, cover, and steam for about 14 minutes, or until opaque throughout.

Heat the peanut oil in a small, heavy saucepan over high heat until smoking. Transfer the moi to warmed plates and garnish with the cilantro. Pour the oil over the fish and serve with the steamed rice.

fresh fillet of moi with peanut crust and kula baby bok choy

Serves 4 as a main course

Joey Macadangdang, executive chef at Roy's Kihei restaurant on Maui, took an old recipe of mine—Lemongrass-Crusted Swordfish with Thai Peanut Sauce—and gave it a whole new delicious twist. The bok choy is grown in Kula, on the slopes of Mount Haleakala, Maui's 10,000-foot volcano. Kula lies mostly between 2,500 and 4,000 feet, where the climate is ideal for growing a wide range of fruit and vegetables, including sweet onions, cabbage, and greens such as bok choy.

Joey's Aromatic Sauce

1 tablespoon sesame oil

1 tablespoon olive oil

3 shallots, finely sliced

5 fresh or frozen kaffir lime leaves

2 stalks lemongrass (white part only), peeled and finely sliced

1 teaspoon red pepper flakes

1 teaspoon sugar

1 tablespoon sweet sherry

1 tablespoon soy sauce

2 tablespoons oyster sauce

1 cup veal stock (page 220) or beef stock

¼ cup canned coconut milk

Peanut Crust and Moi

1 tablespoon smooth peanut butter

1 tablespoon soy sauce

1 large egg

1 teaspoon ground ginger

1 tablespoon minced scallion (green part only)

¼ cup chopped salted peanuts

¼ cup panko (Japanese bread crumbs)

4 moi fillets, about 7 ounces each

Salt and freshly ground black pepper

1 tablespoon unsalted butter

1 tablespoon olive oil

4 small baby bok choy

4 teaspoons scallion oil (page 225)

To prepare the sauce, heat the sesame oil and olive oil in a heavy saucepan over medium-high heat until hot and shimmering. Add the shallots, lime leaves, lemongrass, red pepper flakes, and sugar and stir for about 2 minutes until golden brown. Stir in the sherry and cook to reduce the liquid by half. Add the soy sauce, oyster sauce, and stock and cook to reduce again by half. Add the coconut milk, bring to a boil, decrease the heat, and simmer for 3 minutes longer. Transfer to a blender or food processor and purée until smooth. Strain the sauce into a clean saucepan. Set aside and keep warm.

To prepare the crust and moi, combine the peanut butter, soy sauce, egg, ground ginger, and scallion in a bowl. Whisk until smooth. Combine the salted peanuts and panko on a plate. Stir to blend and set aside. Season the moi with salt and pepper to taste and dip one side of each fillet in the peanut butter crust mixture. Then dip in the panko mixture on the same side.

Melt the butter with the oil in a sauté pan or skillet over medium-high heat. When it begins to foam, add the moi, crust side down. Sauté for about 4 minutes, or until the crust is golden brown. Carefully turn the moi over and cook about 5 minutes longer, or until opaque throughout.

While the moi is cooking, cook the bok choy in a large pot of salted boiling water for 30 seconds. Drain well and place on one side of each warmed plate. Spoon the warm sauce into the center of each plate and arrange the crusted moi on top of the sauce. Garnish the sauce with a drizzle of the scallion oil.

monchong
bigscale or sickle pomfret
(Taractichthys steindachneri)

general description

Monchong is a deep-water fish caught year-round, mostly by longline tuna and snapper fishermen, though usually it is not a specifically targeted species but a welcome and marketable "by-catch" (like opah). Monchong range between 5 and 25 pounds, with the prime size being over 12 pounds.

uses, flavor, and cooking qualities

Much of the commercial monchong catch is sold to restaurants. It is generally sold in fillet form, as the skin is thick and scaly. Monchong has a white flesh with light pink tones, and a firm, moist texture. When cooked, the flesh turns white. Its medium-high fat content helps to give it a defined, straightforward, and very pleasant flavor. It is a versatile fish that takes well to marinades and can be sautéed, steamed, broiled, or grilled. Its texture and flavor also make it a good choice for sashimi, although it is rarely served this way.

substitutions

Other firm-fleshed deep-water fish, such as snapper (opakapaka, onaga, and uku).

monchong recipes

Crisp-Fried Mochiko Monchong with Coconut-Curry
    Sauce | 56

Teriyaki-Grilled Monchong with Wasabi-Daikon
    Vinaigrette | 59

crisp-fried mochiko monchong with coconut-curry sauce

Serves 4 as a main course

Mochiko, or rice flour (available in Japanese or Asian markets), makes a great crust for fish because it gives it an attractively crisp texture. I created this dish to echo the Japanese classic chicken katsu, which is sometimes served with curry sauce. You can use ono, snapper, or any similar thick-fleshed fillets for this dish. I recommend serving it with steamed jasmine rice, basmati rice, or long-grain rice.

Coconut-Curry Sauce

- 2 tablespoons canola oil
- 1 tablespoon minced shallot
- 1 tablespoon minced garlic
- 2 teaspoons minced fresh ginger
- 2 tablespoons minced scallions (white part only)
- ½ cup chicken stock (page 219)
- 2 tablespoons julienned fresh basil
- 1 can (19 ounces) coconut milk
- 2 tablespoons Thai red curry paste
- 3 tablespoons fish sauce
- 2 tablespoons palm sugar
- Salt and freshly ground black pepper
- 1 tablespoon coriander seeds
- ¼ cup minced fresh cilantro
- 1 stalk fresh lemongrass (white part only), peeled and minced
- 4 fresh or frozen kaffir lime leaves, minced

Mochiko Monchong

- 4 cups canola oil
- 1 cup mochiko (rice flour)
- ¾ cup water
- 2 tablespoons fish sauce
- 2 tablespoons freshly squeezed lemon juice
- 1 large egg, beaten
- 1 tablespoon minced garlic
- 1 tablespoon minced fresh ginger
- 1 teaspoon minced fresh or frozen kaffir lime leaf
- 4 (7-ounce) monchong fillets

To prepare the sauce, heat the oil in a large, heavy saucepan over medium-high heat. Add the shallot, garlic, ginger, and scallions and sauté for 1 minute. Add the stock and stir to deglaze the pan. Add the basil, coconut milk, curry paste, fish sauce, palm sugar, salt and pepper to taste, coriander seeds, cilantro, lemongrass, and lime leaves. Bring to a boil, decrease the heat, and simmer for about 5 minutes. Strain the sauce into a clean saucepan and keep warm.

To prepare the monchong, heat the canola oil to 325°F in a deep-fryer or large, heavy saucepan. In a large, shallow bowl, combine the rice flour, water, fish sauce, lemon juice, egg, garlic, ginger, and lime leaf. Mix well to form a smooth batter and

continued

continued
from page 56 dip the fish into the batter to coat thoroughly. Add two of the monchong fillets to the hot oil and deep-fry for about 5 minutes, or until golden brown and cooked through. Remove the fish with tongs, let drain on paper towels, and keep warm. Repeat for the remaining fillets. Spoon the sauce into small dipping bowls and serve the monchong alongside.

teriyaki-grilled monchong with wasabi-daikon vinaigrette

Serves 4 as a main course

The spicy wasabi, pungent daikon, and salty ogo in the vinaigrette provide the perfect contrast to the sweet tones of the teriyaki-infused fish, and the combination successfully echoes the traditional Japanese presentation of grilled fish served with grated daikon. Serve this dish with steamed bok choy or broccolini, or your favorite green vegetable, and steamed rice.

Teriyaki Marinade and Monchong

½ cup soy sauce

½ cup sugar

2 tablespoons minced scallions (including green parts)

1 tablespoon minced garlic

1 tablespoon minced fresh ginger

1 tablespoon white sesame seeds, toasted (page 228)

4 monchong fillets, about 7 ounces each

Wasabi-Daikon Vinaigrette

6 tablespoons soy sauce

6 tablespoons rice vinegar

¼ cup chopped Maui or other sweet white onion

2 tablespoons fresh ogo seaweed

2 tablespoons wasabi paste

¼ cup grated daikon

Prepare a medium-hot fire in a charcoal grill or preheat a gas grill to 450°F.

To prepare the marinade and fish, combine the soy sauce and sugar in a bowl and stir until the sugar dissolves. Stir in the scallions, garlic, ginger, and sesame seeds. Transfer to a shallow glass baking dish and add the fish. Let marinate for 10 minutes, turning once.

While the fish is marinating, prepare the vinaigrette: Combine all the ingredients in a blender. Purée until smooth and set aside.

Remove the monchong from the marinade and grill for about 3 minutes on each side, or until opaque throughout. Transfer to warmed plates and spoon the vinaigrette around the fish.

onaga

long-tailed red snapper or ruby snapper

(Etelis coruscans)

general description

Onaga, like opakapaka, is a variety of snapper (see page 85). They congregate around rocky seafloor outcroppings and drop-offs. They are caught in deep Hawaiian waters, have brilliant red skin, and typically weigh from 1 to more than 10 pounds. In Hawaii, this fish is usually referred to by its Japanese name, onaga, rather than its Hawaiian name, ula'ula, or snapper. One word of warning: In some markets (especially on the West Coast), red rockfish is marketed as Pacific red snapper. There are several types of rockfish, and while some are similar in flavor and texture to onaga, others are noticeably inferior. As true onaga is expensive, try to verify your purchase.

uses, flavors, and cooking qualities

In terms of weight and value, the onaga is the second most important bottom fish landed in Hawaii (opakapaka is the first). Peak season is during the winter, when the fish's higher fat content makes it more suitable for sashimi. Onaga has a white to pale pink flesh that turns white when cooked. Its texture is a little firmer than opakapaka, and it has a delicate, refined flavor. In Hawaii, onaga is popular among the ethnic Asian communities, especially during the winter months and for celebrations and ceremonies such as the New Year. Like opakapaka, it is a versatile fish, and it can be prepared in similar ways (see page 85).

If you are buying onaga whole, avoid those over 3 pounds or so, as these are usually not as tender.

substitutions

Other snappers, particularly opakapaka (pink snapper), gray snapper (uku), and Atlantic red snapper; also sea bass, grouper, and halibut.

onaga recipes

braised onaga in soy, nabemono style

Serves 4 as a main course

In Japanese cuisine, nabemono—literally, "pot thing"—is a traditional style of one-pot cooking; the pot is a stoneware casserole called a *name*. Here, I have combined ramen noodles, which are one of my favorite comfort foods, with a traditional Japanese-style broth and flavorful onaga. You can use salmon steaks, if you prefer, especially if you are concerned about overcooking the onaga; just bear in mind that the flavor of the finished dish will be very different.

Japanese wheat flour noodles are sold fresh or dried in Asian markets. Ramen noodles are often used in ready-made one-pot meals.

Broth

1 cup water

2 teaspoons dashi

3 tablespoons sake

3 tablespoons soy sauce

2 tablespoons mirin

1 tablespoon sugar

Salt and freshly ground black pepper

8 ounces fresh ramen noodles, Chinese egg noodles, or udon noodles

4 (6-ounce) onaga fillets

8 shiitake mushroom caps

1 scallion, finely sliced (including green parts)

2 baby bok choy, julienned

Garnish

2 tablespoons minced red pickled ginger

1 tablespoon white sesame seeds, toasted (see page 228)

To prepare the broth, pour the water into a large Japanese *name*-style stoneware casserole or other heatproof casserole and add the dashi, sake, soy sauce, mirin, sugar, and salt and pepper to taste. Bring the broth to a boil over high heat.

Add the ramen noodles to the broth and carefully arrange the onaga on top of the noodles. Place 2 shiitake caps on top of each fish and sprinkle with the scallion. Top with the bok choy and cover the casserole. Decrease the heat to low and cook for 4 to 5 minutes until the onaga is opaque throughout.

Serve the casserole at the table family style, using individual serving bowls. Garnish each serving with the pickled ginger and sesame seeds.

basil-scented onaga with waimanalo sweet corn and asparagus risotto

Serves 4 as a main course

The preparation for the onaga in this recipe, which makes for an attractive presentation, can also be used for mahimahi, snapper, or other firm-fleshed white fish. In putting together the flavors for the risotto, I was swayed by the winning combination of two ingredients I love to use: fresh, young local asparagus from Waialua, on Oahu's North Shore, grown by Dean Okimoto, and tender Waimanalo corn, also grown for Roy's by Dean on the island's windward side.

Risotto

- 3 tablespoons unsalted butter, plus 4 tablespoons butter, softened
- 2 tablespoons canola oil
- 2 shallots, minced
- 2 cups Japanese short-grain rice
- 3 cups chicken stock (page 219), plus more as needed
- ¼ cup corn kernels (about 1 ear)
- ¼ cup sliced asparagus
- 2 tablespoons diced tomato
- 2 tablespoons diced shiitake mushroom caps
- Salt and freshly ground black pepper

Basil-Scented Onaga

- 2 tablespoons unsalted butter
- 4 large fresh basil leaves
- 4 (7-ounce) onaga fillets
- Salt and freshly ground black pepper

- 4 fresh basil leaves, for garnish

To prepare the risotto, melt the 3 tablespoons butter with the oil in a saucepan over medium-high heat. Add the shallots and sauté for 1 to 2 minutes, or until translucent. Add the rice and stir for 1 minute. Add the 3 cups stock, bring to a simmer, and decrease the heat to medium-low. Stir constantly with a wooden spoon for 15 to 20 minutes, or until the liquid is just absorbed. Add the corn, asparagus, tomato, and mushrooms and continue to cook, adding more stock if necessary, 5 to 10 minutes longer, or until the rice is al dente and the vegetables are tender. Season with salt and pepper to taste and stir in the 4 tablespoons butter to finish.

Meanwhile, prepare the onaga: Melt the 2 tablespoons butter in a nonstick sauté pan or skillet set over medium-high heat. Place a basil leaf on each fillet, season with salt and pepper to taste, and sauté for about 2 minutes on each side, or until opaque throughout. Spoon the risotto onto each warmed serving plate and smooth out to make a bed for the fish. Arrange the onaga fillets on top of the risotto. Garnish each with a fresh basil leaf.

cassoulet of onaga with pancetta, farro, shiitake mushrooms, and baby kale

Serves 4 as a main course

This rustic-style recipe features farro, an ancient grain that sustained Mediterranean cultures—the Roman Empire in particular—over thousands of years. In ground form, it was the original ingredient for polenta, a staple of the region for centuries before cornmeal arrived from the New World. Farro is similar to spelt, which can be used as an alternative in this recipe, as can barley. I first tasted farro at my restaurant in Pebble Beach, when Executive Chef Elias Lopez put it on the menu as a starch to accompany onaga. It adds a hearty touch to any fish dish, and because of its brown color, I prefer to match it with a contrasting white-fleshed fish such as mahimahi, ono, or snapper.

12 Brussels sprouts, trimmed and halved	1½ cups coarsely chopped baby kale or cabbage
3½ cups chicken stock (page 219)	1 tomato, cut into 16 thin slices
6 ounces farro or barley	2 tablespoons dry white wine
2 tablespoons extra-virgin olive oil	2 tablespoons soy sauce
¼ cup minced pancetta	Salt and freshly ground black pepper
1 tablespoon minced garlic	¼ cup olive oil
½ tablespoon seeded and minced red Thai chile	4 (6-ounce) onaga fillets
½ cup diced shiitake mushroom caps	1 teaspoon minced fresh thyme
1 tablespoon minced shallot	1 teaspoon minced fresh basil

Prepare an ice bath in a large bowl. Score the stem end of each Brussels sprout with an X. Cook the sprouts in a saucepan of salted boiling water for 2 to 3 minutes until crisp-tender. Drain the sprouts and transfer immediately to the ice bath to stop the cooking process. When cool, drain again and set aside.

Bring the stock to a boil over high heat in a saucepan and add the farro. Cook for about 10 minutes, or until tender. Drain and set the farro aside.

Heat the extra-virgin olive oil in a sauté pan or skillet over medium-high heat. Add the pancetta, garlic, chile, mushrooms, and shallot and sauté for about 1 minute. Add the cooked farro and sprouts, the cabbage, and tomato slices, and continue to cook for 1½ minutes. Add the wine and stir to scrape the browned bits from the bottom of the pan. Season with the soy sauce and salt and pepper to taste. Set aside and keep warm.

Heat the olive oil in a stainless-steel sauté pan or skillet over medium-high heat. Place the onaga fillets on a large plate, coat on one side with the thyme and basil, and season with salt and pepper to taste on both sides. Transfer the onaga to the hot pan and cook for about 3 minutes on each side or until opaque throughout.

To serve, transfer the farro mixture to warmed pasta bowls and carefully place the cooked onaga on top.

cilantro-and-sesame-crusted onaga with sake-mango vinaigrette

Serves 4 as a main course

Onaga is another fish that takes well to crusting, and this crust recipe also works well with mahimahi, opakapaka, and other firm, white-fleshed fish. In this lighter-style dish, I have paired the delicate, crusted onaga with an intense, fruity sauce. The herbal tones of the cilantro, the hint of fresh ginger, and the kick provided by the gingery sake make it a sauce you will want to serve with other fish. I like to partner this dish with steamed green beans and steamed rice, but feel free to serve with your favorite sides.

Vinaigrette

1 cup mango purée

2 tablespoons sake

1 ½ tablespoons freshly squeezed lemon juice

1 teaspoon ginger juice (page 231)

Salt and freshly ground black pepper

Onaga

1 tablespoon minced fresh cilantro

1 ½ tablespoons white sesame seeds, toasted (page 228)

1 teaspoon minced garlic

1 teaspoon minced fresh ginger

⅛ teaspoon shichimi

4 onaga fillets, about 7 ounces each

Salt and freshly ground black pepper

¼ cup olive oil

To prepare the vinaigrette, pour the mango purée into a bowl and stir in the sake, lemon juice, ginger juice, and salt and pepper to taste. Mix thoroughly and set aside.

To prepare the fish, combine the cilantro and sesame seeds in a bowl and stir in the garlic, ginger, and shichimi. Coat the onaga with the mixture on one side only and season with salt and pepper on both sides. Heat the olive oil into a nonstick sauté pan or skillet over medium-high heat until hot and shimmering. Add the onaga, crust side down, and sauté for about 2 minutes. Carefully turn over with a spatula and sauté the other side for about 3 minutes, or until the fish is opaque throughout.

Ladle the vinaigrette onto warmed serving plates and place the onaga on top.

ono

wahoo, tigerfish, or oceanic barracuda

(Acanthocybium solandri)

general description

Probably the most elegant member of the mackerel family, and one of the largest, ono usually weigh between 10 and 30 pounds when landed, although some grow much larger (over 100 pounds). Ono live in open tropical or warm waters worldwide, and especially around Hawaii and in the Caribbean (where they are considered a gamefish); they often congregate around ocean seamounts. Most are caught by trolling or by longline fishing, and peak season for ono is summer and fall. Fast swimmers, ono migrate large distances. The name *wahoo,* which is more commonly used on the mainland United States, is supposedly derived from the early European explorers' pronunciation of the Hawaiian island of Oahu, where they found the fish to be plentiful. (Another colorful theory is that fishermen yelled "wahoo!" when the fish took the lure.)

uses, flavor, and cooking qualities

Ono has pale pink to white flesh that turns white when cooked, with a firm, slightly coarse texture. Its medium fat content tends to keep the texture moist, but it is prone to drying out if at all overcooked. Ono is the most delicately flavored member of the mackerel family, with sweet tones (*ono* means "sweet" or "good to eat" in Hawaiian), sometimes compared to those of mahimahi or albacore tuna (tombo). Ono is usually sold in fillet form. It is versatile and can be grilled, sautéed, broiled, poached, or baked. It takes well to crusts and batters, which help prevent it from drying out. Due to its fat content, ono is also favored for sashimi.

substitutions

Most firm-fleshed fish, especially grouper, sea bass, snapper, mahimahi, and halibut.

ono recipes

crisp pan-fried ono with yuzu-soy vinaigrette

Serves 4 as a main course

In this recipe, the ono is deep-fried in a traditional Japanese style that is typically used for chicken, although here, I have added some fresh lemon juice to the marinade. The yuzu in the vinaigrette is a Japanese citrus (see page 235); if unavailable, substitute ¼ cup fresh lemon juice mixed with ¼ cup orange juice. Serve this dish with rice, steamed baby bok choy or snap peas, or your favorite vegetable. Another variation I make on this recipe to create a delicious appetizer—or for a party dish—is to dice about 1 pound of ono, marinate it the same way, and then to toss it with 2 cups of cornstarch and ¼ cup of shichimi togarashi. Make sure the fish is completely coated, deep-fry it, and serve with the yuzu vinaigrette as a dipping sauce.

Marinade and Fish

- ½ cup soy sauce
- ¼ cup freshly squeezed lemon juice
- 3 tablespoons sake
- 1½ tablespoons ginger juice (see page 231)
- 3 tablespoons sugar
- ¼ cup finely sliced scallions (including green parts)
- 4 (7-ounce) ono fillets

Vinaigrette

- ½ cup yuzu juice
- ½ cup soy sauce
- 2 tablespoons olive oil
- 2 tablespoons peanut oil
- 2 tablespoons sugar
- ¼ cup grated fresh ginger
- 2 tablespoons minced onion chives or regular chives

- 4 cups canola oil
- 4 large egg whites
- 1 cup cornstarch, for dusting
- Salt and freshly ground black pepper

To prepare the marinade and fish, combine the soy sauce, lemon juice, sake, and ginger juice in a bowl. Add the sugar and whisk until it dissolves, then whisk in the scallions. Add the ono and marinate for 15 to 20 minutes, turning once.

While the ono is marinating, prepare the vinaigrette. Combine the yuzu, soy sauce, olive oil, and peanut oil in a bowl. Add the sugar and whisk until it dissolves. Whisk in the ginger and chives. Set aside.

Heat the canola oil to 375°F in a deep fryer or large, heavy saucepan. In a bowl, whisk the egg whites until frothy. Remove the ono from the marinade and dip into

continued

continued
from page 71 the egg whites. Dust the ono with cornstarch and season with salt and pepper to taste. Transfer the ono to the hot oil and deep-fry for about 4 minutes, or until golden brown. Remove the fish with tongs and arrange on warmed plates. Drizzle the vinaigrette around the ono and serve.

crisp pan-fried ono with pineapple vegetables and a sweet and sour black vinegar sauce

Serves 4 as a main course

I created this dish after a trip to Beijing, which is where I first tasted black vinegar, made from glutinous rice, millet, or sorghum, and malt. I love using it for both its rich, complex, and slightly smoky flavor and its dark color; the best ones are aged for years, like balsamic vinegar. On the same trip, I enjoyed some fabulous sweet and sour sauces, and once I returned home, I decided that this combination of ingredients would be a natural match for a fish like ono. To give the recipe a distinctive Hawaiian touch, as well as an unusual twist and a little more sweetness, I added pineapple to the vegetable mixture.

Marinade and Fish

4 large eggs

4 tablespoons soy sauce

2 tablespoons cornstarch

1 tablespoon grated fresh ginger

1 tablespoon grated garlic

4 (7-ounce) ono fillets

Sweet and Sour Sauce

¼ cup Chinese black vinegar

2 tablespoons soy sauce

¼ cup sugar

Vegetables

¼ cup sesame oil

1 teaspoon minced garlic

1 teaspoon grated fresh ginger

½ Maui or other sweet white onion, julienned

1 red bell pepper, seeded, deribbed, and cut into 1-inch diamonds

1 yellow bell pepper, seeded, deribbed, and cut into 1-inch diamonds

2 baby bok choy, halved lengthwise and julienned

¼ cup diced fresh pineapple

2 tablespoons cornstarch mixed with 2 tablespoons warm water

2 tablespoons sesame oil

4 fresh cilantro sprigs, for garnish

To prepare the marinade and fish, whisk the eggs in a bowl until blended, then whisk in the soy sauce, cornstarch, ginger, and garlic. Put the ono in a shallow dish and pour the marinade over. Refrigerate for 15 to 20 minutes.

Meanwhile, prepare the sauce and vegetables. Combine the vinegar and soy sauce in a bowl and whisk in the sugar until it dissolves. Set aside.

Heat the sesame oil in a large, heavy sauté pan or skillet over medium-high heat until hot and shimmering. Add the garlic, ginger, onion, bell peppers, and bok choy and sauté for 2 to 3 minutes, until the bok choy softens. Add the pineapple and sauté 1 minute longer. Stir in the sweet and sour sauce, then the cornstarch mixture. Cook, stirring, for 2 to 3 minutes, or until thickened. Set aside and keep warm.

Remove the ono from the marinade. Heat the sesame oil in a large, heavy nonstick sauté pan or skillet over medium-high heat. Add the ono and sauté for 2 to 3 minutes on each side, until opaque throughout.

Transfer the vegetable mixture to warmed plates and top with the ono. Garnish with the cilantro sprigs.

crab-and-potato-crusted ono with creamed spinach and bacon

Serves 4 as a main course

I have been using a crabmeat and potato crust on fish for several years, and it has become a firm favorite with our guests. Ono tends to be dry in texture, so the crust helps to retain its natural moisture; deep-frying is another good cooking method for ono, for the same reason. The spinach and bacon make this a hearty dish with plenty of robust flavors.

Ono

½ cup warm mashed potatoes (page 226)

½ cup fresh lump crabmeat, picked over for shell

1 tablespoon julienned fresh basil

Salt and freshly ground black pepper

4 (7-ounce) ono fillets

1 tablespoon canola oil

Creamed Spinach and Bacon

3 slices bacon

1 teaspoon minced shallot

1 teaspoon minced garlic

12 ounces spinach, washed and steamed

1 cup heavy cream

Salt and freshly ground black pepper

4 carrots, peeled, thinly sliced, and blanched

Fresh basil leaves, for garnish

To prepare the ono, put the mashed potatoes in a bowl. Add the crabmeat, basil, and salt and pepper to taste and stir to thoroughly combine. Spread the mixture on one side of each ono fillet to form a crust. Heat the oil in a heavy nonstick sauté pan or skillet over medium heat. Add the ono, crust side down, and sauté for 3 minutes, until the crust turns golden brown. Turn the fillet over and sauté for about 2 minutes longer, or until opaque throughout.

To prepare the spinach, heat a dry heavy sauté pan or skillet over medium heat for 2 minutes. Add the bacon and sauté for 4 to 5 minutes, until crisp. Remove and mince the bacon; set aside. Drain off all but 1 teaspoon of the bacon fat and increase the heat to medium-high. Add the shallot and garlic. Immediately add the spinach and cook until it begins to wilt. Transfer to a colander and press with the back of a wooden spoon to release excess moisture. Chop the spinach and set aside. Pour the cream into a saucepan and bring to a boil. Cook to reduce the cream by about two-thirds or until thickened and pastelike. Add the spinach and cook for about 1 minute. Season with salt and pepper to taste. Set aside and keep warm.

In the center of warmed serving plates, arrange the blanched carrots and top with the creamed spinach. Place the crusted ono on top of the spinach. Garnish the ono with the bacon and basil.

opah

moonfish

(Lampris regius)

general description

Opah is an extraordinary-looking ocean fish, with an almost perfectly round shape; a comparatively thin, flat profile; a silvery skin, and bright crimson fins. When mature, it is large, reaching up to 200 pounds, although those landed in Hawaii typically weigh less, averaging around 100 pounds. Opah prefers to live on the slopes of ocean seamounts in the warm waters around Hawaii, and it is a solitary, nonschooling fish. Since it is not a targeted species (like monchong), it is usually a by-catch, but it is a prized species for eating. Although caught year-round, opah is most common between April and August. It is regarded by Hawaiians as a fish that brings good luck, and so is often given away by private fishermen as a gesture of goodwill. Another type of closely related moonfish (*Lampris guttatus*) is caught in the Atlantic.

The pink to orange flesh of opah turns white when cooked. It has a fine, soft, yet dense texture and is sold in fillet or steak form. It has a medium, rich flavor. As the flesh has a relatively low fat content, opah is best sautéed, steamed, baked, or poached, but it can also be successfully grilled over medium heat.

substitutions

Swordfish and tuna.

opah recipes

Herb-Crusted Opah with Grilled Portobello
  Mushroom–Garlic Sauce | 79

Grilled Opah Steaks with a Green Papaya and Hearts of
  Palm Salad | 81

Goat-Cheese-and-Spinach-Crusted Opah with
  Red Wine Sauce | 82

roy's fish and seafood

herb-crusted opah with grilled portobello mushroom—garlic sauce

Serves 4 as a main course

Contrasts in flavors, textures, and/or colors often make a particular dish stand out, which is the case here. The hearty mushrooms in the sauce have a meaty texture and rich, deep flavor that contrast with the delicate, herbal quality of the fish, yet the two are entirely complementary. I will admit that I am not a great fan of portobellos, but plenty of my guests are, and this is a very popular dish at my restaurants. I recommend serving it with mashed potatoes and steamed asparagus.

Grilled Portobello Mushroom–Garlic Sauce

2 tablespoons olive oil

1 tablespoon minced garlic

2 tablespoons minced shallots

1 cup sliced portobello mushroom

¼ cup dry white wine

2 tablespoons julienned fresh basil

½ cup canned coconut milk

½ cup demi-glace (page 221)

¼ cup chicken stock (page 219)

Salt and freshly ground black pepper

Herb-Crusted Opah

1 tablespoon minced fresh basil

1 tablespoon minced fresh thyme

2 teaspoons minced garlic

4 (7-ounce) opah fillets

Salt and freshly ground black pepper

2 tablespoons olive oil

To prepare the sauce, heat the oil in a heavy saucepan over medium-high heat. Add the garlic, shallots, and mushroom, and sauté for about 3 minutes, until the portobello is soft. Stir in the wine. Immediately add the basil, coconut milk, demi-glace, stock, and salt and pepper to taste. Bring to a boil. Cook to reduce the sauce for 2 to 3 minutes, until it thickens and coats the back of a spoon. Set aside and keep warm.

To prepare the opah, combine the basil, thyme, and garlic in a bowl and stir to blend. Coat the opah on one side with the mixture and season with salt and pepper to taste on both sides. Heat the oil in a heavy stainless-steel sauté pan or skillet over medium-high heat until almost smoking. Add the opah, crust side down, and sauté for 2 to 3 minutes. Turn over and sauté 2 minutes longer, until opaque throughout.

Transfer the opah to warmed plates and spoon the sauce around the fish.

grilled opah steaks with a green papaya and hearts of palm salad

Serves 4 as a main course

Sliced green papayas are used to make a classic Thai-style salad, and I have added a twist with the addition of fresh hearts of palm. As Elizabeth Schneider explains in her encyclopedic book, *Vegetables: From Amaranth to Zucchini* (William Morrow, 2001), the "hearts" are actually "crunchy-creamy terminal buds (growing tips) from which the new leaves will emerge." Most of the fresh hearts of palm available in the United States are harvested from the peach palm, and our supplier is on the Big Island of Hawaii. If fresh hearts are unavailable, use cooked artichoke hearts, as canned or jarred hearts of palm will not have the same flavor.

Salad

1 green papaya, peeled, seeded, and julienned

6 ounces haricots verts or baby Blue Lake green beans, trimmed

1 cup julienned fresh hearts of palm, or 4 cooked artichoke hearts, julienned

1 tomato, thinly sliced

Dressing

2 tablespoons olive oil

1 tablespoon minced garlic

1 teaspoon minced dried shrimp

2 Thai red chiles, seeded and minced

2 tablespoons fish sauce

2 tablespoons sugar

Salt and freshly ground black pepper

Opah

4 (7-ounce) opah steaks

1 tablespoon minced garlic

1 tablespoon minced fresh cilantro

Salt and freshly ground black pepper

Garnish

4 fresh cilantro sprigs

1 red bell pepper, deribbed, seeded, and julienned

Prepare a medium-hot fire in a charcoal grill, or preheat a gas grill to 450°F.

To prepare the salad, soak the julienned papaya in a bowl of cold salted water for 30 minutes. Meanwhile, prepare an ice bath in a large bowl. In a large saucepan of salted boiling water, cook the beans for 2 to 3 minutes, or until just crisp-tender. Drain and transfer to the ice bath to stop the cooking process. Drain again and transfer to a bowl. Drain the papaya and add to the bowl with the hearts of palm. Add the tomato, gently toss together, and refrigerate while preparing the dressing.

continued

continued
from page 81
To prepare the dressing, heat the oil in a small saucepan over medium-high heat. Add the garlic and sauté for 2 to 3 minutes, until light golden brown. Stir in the dried shrimp and chiles and sauté 1 minute longer. Stir in the fish sauce and add the sugar. Stir until the sugar dissolves and season with salt and pepper to taste. Set aside and keep warm.

Coat the opah steaks on both sides with the garlic and cilantro and season with salt and pepper to taste. Transfer to the grill and cook for 2 to 3 minutes on each side, or until opaque throughout.

Pour the warm dressing over the salad and toss to coat. Transfer to plates and arrange the opah steaks on top of the salad. Garnish with the cilantro and red pepper.

goat-cheese-and-spinach-crusted opah with red wine sauce

Serves 4 as a main course

The flavorful crust for the opah is based on a popular goat cheese and mascarpone dip I created for a completely different dish a few years ago. A little later, it occurred to me that combining the dip ingredients with spinach and garlic would make a great way to crust fish and preserve its natural moistness. The walnuts and red wine in the sauce are natural partners with the cheese crust, and the contrasting textures of the ingredients have helped to boost the popularity of this dish. Serve with mashed or boiled potatoes.

Red Wine Sauce

½ cup dry red wine

½ cup demi-glace (page 221)

¼ cup chopped walnuts, toasted (page 228)

Crust

2 tablespoons olive oil

1 tablespoon minced garlic

2 cups packed chopped spinach

¼ cup soft goat cheese

¼ cup mascarpone

¼ cup sour cream

Salt and freshly ground black pepper

Garnish

Canola oil, for frying

½ cup all-purpose flour

¼ cup thinly sliced shallots

Opah

¼ cup olive oil

4 (7-ounce) opah fillets

Salt and freshly ground black pepper

To prepare the sauce, combine the red wine and demi-glace in a saucepan. Bring just to a simmer over medium heat and decrease the heat to low. Cook to reduce the sauce until it is thick enough to coat the back of a spoon. Stir in the toasted walnuts. Set aside and keep warm.

To prepare the crust, heat the 2 tablespoons olive oil in a sauté pan or skillet over medium-high heat. Add the garlic and spinach and sauté for about 1 minute, or until the spinach is wilted. Set aside to cool. In a bowl, combine the goat cheese, mascarpone, and sour cream. Stir to blend. When the spinach is cool enough to handle, gently squeeze out the excess moisture and combine with the cheese mixture. Season with salt and pepper to taste and set aside.

Preheat the broiler. To prepare the garnish, heat 1 inch of canola oil in a heavy saucepan over medium-high heat. Put the flour in a bowl, add the shallots, and toss to coat. Transfer to a sieve and shake it to remove the excess flour. Add the shallots to the pan and fry for 1 to 2 minutes, until crisp. Remove with a slotted spoon and drain on paper towels.

To prepare the opah, heat the 1/4 cup olive oil in a large, heavy sauté pan or skillet over medium-high heat. Lightly season the opah with salt and pepper to taste and sear for 15 seconds on each side. Remove the opah from the pan and spread the goat cheese mixture on one side of each fillet. Transfer the fillets, crust side up, to a baking dish or roasting pan and broil for 8 to 10 minutes, until the crust is bubbling and the opah is opaque throughout.

To serve, place the opah fillets on warmed plates and spoon the sauce around the fish. Garnish with the crisp shallots.

opakapaka

pink snapper or
crimson jobfish

(Pristimoides filamentosus)

general description

There are numerous species of snapper, many of which are some shade of pink or red. Snappers are so-called because they have sharp teeth, which they snap assertively when caught. Snapper is found worldwide in tropical and subtropical ocean waters. The opakapaka, caught in deep Hawaiian waters, prefers rocky seafloor drop-offs, usually at depths of 250 to 750 feet. It has pink to light brown skin and typically weighs from 1 to 5 pounds.

uses, flavor, and cooking qualities

Opakapaka has a delicate, flaky, but moist and firm texture, qualities that make it the premium snapper in Hawaiian cuisine. Visitors to Hawaii in particular seem to appreciate opakapaka, and those visiting Roy's often tell me it is the favorite fish they have tasted during their stay. Its flesh is white to pale pink and turns bright white when cooked. Opakapaka are generally lean fish with low fat content, although they tend to be somewhat fattier in winter, when they are more abundant. The flesh has a slightly sweet, delicate flavor. Opakapaka is a very versatile fish that can be prepared in a variety of ways: baked, grilled, sautéed, poached, or steamed. It is sometimes served raw for sashimi (especially in winter).

substitutions

Other snappers, particularly gray snapper (uku) and Hawaiian red snapper (onaga); black cod, halibut, sea bass, and grouper.

opakapaka recipes

pan-seared opakapaka with lobster-truffle sauce and kabayaki drizzle

Serves 4 as a main course

One of my favorite combinations is opakapaka with lobster sauce, and it's a pairing I've served since Roy's first opened in Honolulu in 1988. It's a popular tradition that I'm not about to mess with! Kabayaki sauce (page 231) makes a great taste match with the truffles in this fusion dish; you can find the sauce in Asian stores or in the Asian condiment section of larger supermarkets. Serve with steamed rice (page 227), Happy Rice (page 90), mashed potatoes (page 226), or your favorite accompaniment.

Lobster-Truffle Sauce

1 cup warm beurre blanc (page 223)

1 tablespoon lobster paste (page 224)

1 tablespoon truffle oil

Opakapaka fillets

4 (7-ounce) opakapaka fillets

Salt and freshly ground black pepper

¼ cup canola oil

¼ cup kabayaki sauce

To prepare the lobster-truffle sauce, combine the beurre blanc, lobster paste, and truffle oil. Stir to blend. Set aside and keep warm over barely simmering water.

Place the opakapaka on a large plate, season with salt and pepper to taste, and coat with the oil. Heat a dry stainless-steel sauté pan or skillet over medium-high heat for 2 to 3 minutes. Add the opakapaka, skin side down. Sear for about 2 minutes while holding the fillets down with a spatula so the skin does not curl up (you will find this easier if you sear only 2 fillets at a time). Turn over and sear the other side for about 2 minutes or until opaque throughout.

To serve, transfer the opakapaka to serving plates and pour the lobster sauce around the fish. Drizzle the kabayaki sauce over the lobster sauce.

sesame seed–crusted steamed opakapaka with lobster-red miso broth

Serves 4 as a main course

This recipe is an updated version of a traditional Japanese miso dish. I never need much of an excuse to use miso, as it was one of my favorite foods growing up in Japan. The saltier, richer red miso is often paired with shellfish in Japanese cuisine, and I recommend using a good-quality miso paste, which will be reflected in the results. Here, I have given the classic ingredient a fusion twist by adapting it for a rich, buttery lobster sauce. The small golden Japanese nameko mushrooms, available in Asian markets, have an okralike gelatinous quality that helps thicken the broth; you can substitute any other type of mushroom, but the texture of the broth will be thinner. Use fresh water chestnuts, if available at Asian markets, or use canned, which are stocked in the Chinese food section of most supermarkets. This preparation also works very well for any type of snapper, sea bass, or grouper.

Lobster-Red Miso Broth

3 cups water

½ cup bonito flakes

¼ cup dashi

¼ cup red miso (aka miso)

8 ounces firm tofu, diced

⅓ cup julienned shiitake mushroom caps

2 tablespoons julienned fresh or canned water chestnuts

½ cup dried wakame seaweed, soaked in cold water for 15 minutes and drained

½ cup fresh or canned nameko mushrooms or diced fresh shiitake caps

6 tablespoons warm beurre blanc (page 223)

½ cup lobster paste (page 224)

Opakapaka

4 (6-ounce) opakapaka fillets

½ tablespoon black sesame seeds, toasted (page 228)

½ tablespoon white sesame seeds, toasted (page 228)

Garnish

1 bunch fresh chives, minced

1 teaspoon tobiko caviar

1 cup mixed baby salad greens

2 cups daikon sprouts

1 tablespoon freshly squeezed lemon juice

1 tablespoon soy sauce

1 package (about 3 ounces) enoki mushrooms

To prepare the broth, pour the water into a saucepan and bring to a boil. Add the bonito flakes and dashi, turn off the heat, and let steep for 30 minutes. Strain the broth through a fine-mesh sieve into a clean saucepan and set over medium-high heat. Add the miso and stir until dissolved. Add the tofu, shiitakes, water chestnuts, wakame, and nameko, and cook for about 5 minutes, or until the shiitakes are cooked through. Whisk in the beurre blanc and lobster paste. Set aside and keep warm.

Add 1 inch of water to a steamer and bring to a boil. Place the opakapaka fillets on a plate and sprinkle the black and white sesame seeds over. Transfer to the steamer, cover, and steam for 3 to 4 minutes, or until the fish is opaque throughout.

While the fish is steaming, prepare the garnish by combining the chives, tobiko, baby greens, and sprouts in a bowl. Sprinkle the lemon juice and soy sauce over, add the enoki mushrooms, and toss to combine.

Ladle about ½ cup of the broth into one of 4 warmed pasta bowls. Add the fish and top with the garnish.

macadamia nut–crusted opakapaka with lobster curry sauce and happy rice

Serves 4 as a main course

Crusting fish with herbs, spices, nuts, seeds, and other ingredients such as potatoes or batter is a technique that has grown in popularity over the last decade or so. Crusting not only provides additional flavor and texture, but also helps to preserve the moistness of the fish. I have featured crusted fish at Roy's since we first opened, and this is another classic dish that dates from Day One. The rich curry sauce provides a new dimension to the opakapaka, and it takes me back to my childhood when my dad would prepare homemade curries. You can substitute any snapper, sea bass, or grouper for the opakapaka in this recipe.

Although relatively expensive, I like the rich flavor of macadamia nut oil. It has a high smoking point, which makes it ideal for cooking at high temperatures.

Lobster Curry Sauce

3 lobster heads and shells, chopped

¼ cup chopped bacon

½ cup chopped celery

½ cup peeled and chopped carrot

½ cup chopped yellow onion

1 tablespoon tomato paste

2 tablespoons Thai red curry paste

1 tablespoon palm sugar

1 tablespoon minced fresh basil

5 cups water

1 teaspoon minced ginger

2 cups canned coconut milk

1 tablespoon fish sauce, or to taste

Salt and freshly ground black pepper

Happy Rice

2 cups steamed rice (page 227)

1 tablespoon minced fresh ginger

1 tablespoon furikake

Macadamia Nut Crust and Opakapaka

2 tablespoons macadamia nut halves

8 tablespoons (1 stick) unsalted butter, softened

¼ cup panko Japanese (bread crumbs)

1 teaspoon macadamia nut oil (optional)

1 teaspoon minced fresh flat-leaf parsley (optional)

1 teaspoon minced fresh lemon thyme (optional)

Pinch of freshly ground white pepper (optional)

4 (7-ounce) opakapaka fillets

4 to 8 fresh chervil or flat-leaf parsley sprigs, for garnish

Preheat the oven to 350°F. To prepare the sauce, place the lobster heads and shells in a roasting pan and roast in the oven for 20 minutes. Put the bacon in a large, heavy saucepan and fry over medium heat for 2 to 3 minutes until lightly browned. Add the celery, carrot, and onion and sauté for about 5 minutes longer, or until the onion is translucent. Add the roasted lobster heads and shells and the tomato paste, curry paste, palm sugar, basil, and water. Decrease the heat to a low simmer and cook 30 minutes longer. Add the ginger and coconut milk and continue to

continued

continued
from page 90 cook over low heat for 30 to 40 minutes. Pass through a medium-fine sieve into a clean saucepan, pressing down on the solids with the back of a wooden spoon to extract as much of the liquid as possible. Season with fish sauce and salt and pepper to taste. Set aside and keep warm.

To prepare the rice, combine all the ingredients. Use small cookie cutters to form the rice into compact shapes. Alternatively, dip your fingers in a bowl of slightly salted water to prevent the rice from sticking and mold 1 to 2 tablespoons of rice into triangles, cubes, or balls. Set aside and keep warm.

To prepare the crust, combine the macadamia nuts, 6 tablespoons of the butter, and the panko in a food processor. Process for 30 seconds until blended. Stir in the macadamia nut oil, parsley, lemon thyme, and pepper. Place the opakapaka on a large plate and spread the crust over one side of each fillet. Melt 1 tablespoon of the remaining butter in a nonstick skillet over medium heat and add 2 fillets, crusted side down. Sear for 4 minutes, then turn over. Cook for 2 to 3 minutes longer, or until opaque throughout. Set aside and keep warm. Repeat to cook the remaining fillets.

To serve, spoon the sauce into the center of warmed serving plates. Top with the opakapaka, crust side up, garnish with the chervil, and serve with the rice.

opakapaka with lobster mash and lobster–pinot noir sauce

Serves 4 as a main course

The mild, sweet flavor of opakapaka, with its moist yet flaky texture, lends itself to rich cream sauces—in this case, my lighter version of the classic red wine bordelaise sauce. Once again, I have chosen to pair the fish with the flavor of lobster because the two go so well together. The mash makes a great side dish for any fish, as well as for chicken and beef.

Lobster–Pinot Noir Sauce

¼ cup canola oil	4 sprigs thyme
1 pound lobster shells, chopped	1 bay leaf
¼ cup peeled and sliced carrot	1 cup pinot noir wine
¼ cup sliced celery	1¼ cups demi-glace (page 221)
2 cloves garlic, sliced	1 cup lobster-dashi stock (page 222)
1 shallot, minced	

Lobster Mash

      8 ounces cooked lobster meat, diced

      2 cups warm mashed potatoes (page 226)

Opakapaka

      4 (6-ounce) opakapaka fillets

      1 teaspoon minced fresh thyme

      1 teaspoon minced fresh basil

      Salt and freshly ground black pepper

      ¼ cup canola oil

To prepare the sauce, heat the canola oil in a large saucepan over medium-high heat. Add the lobster shells and sauté for about 3 minutes, until they turn red. Add the carrot, celery, garlic, shallot, thyme, and bay leaf and sauté 2 minutes longer. Add the wine and stir to deglaze the pan. Cook to reduce the liquid by half. Add the demi-glace and lobster-dashi stock and bring to a simmer. Decrease the heat to low and cook for about 10 minutes until thick enough to coat the back of a spoon. Strain the sauce through a medium-fine sieve into a clean saucepan. Set aside and keep warm.

To prepare the lobster mash, fold the lobster into the mashed potatoes.

To prepare the opakapaka, season the fish on both sides with the thyme, basil, and salt and pepper to taste. Heat the oil in a sauté pan or skillet over medium-high heat until almost smoking. Add the fish and sauté for about 3 minutes on each side, or until opaque throughout.

To serve, spoon the sauce onto warmed plates and place the fish on top of the sauce. Serve with the lobster mash on the side.

pacific salmon

king, sockeye, coho, pink, chum

(Etelis coruscans)

general description

Salmon are abundant in temperate waters in both the northern and southern Pacific, with one-third to one-half of the annual catch being made in Alaskan waters. Pacific salmon are closely related to Atlantic salmon, which are similarly widespread in both hemispheres but low in numbers and considered an endangered species (most Atlantic salmon is now farm-raised, sometimes in ocean enclosures). Pacific salmon, which are mostly caught in the wild, are strong swimmers and are usually found close to the ocean surface. Pacific salmon hatch in fast-flowing freshwater streams and rivers, migrate to the ocean, and then, one to five years later (depending on the species), return to the same freshwater locations to spawn—and, unless they are caught on the way, to die. Peak season for Pacific salmon is summer, with significant catches in the spring and fall. During the winter, farm-raised salmon is increasingly available; however, recent research suggests that farm-raised salmon is significantly less healthful than wild salmon.

uses, flavor, and cooking qualities

Pacific salmon is sold whole (usually up to 4 or 5 pounds) and in steak and fillet form, as well as smoked and canned. It also freezes well. Its flesh ranges in color from white (chum salmon) to pale pink, dark pink, orange (most salmon species), and deep red (king salmon). Its color lends itself to impressive visual presentations on the plate. The relatively high fat content of most types of salmon keeps its texture moist, provided it is not overcooked. The edible skin, which needs to be scaled, is also delicious. The distinctive rich flavor and firm texture of wild salmon make it one of the great eating fish, and it is a particularly good source of omega-3 fatty acids, which are believed to provide positive health benefits for the heart, brain, skin, and joints.

Note that salmon fillets usually contain a row of pin bones, which should be removed with tweezers or pliers. Some salmon steaks will also contain pin bones, which can be removed from the side of the steaks. While salmon skin is good to eat, make sure the scales have been removed, or do it yourself with a fish scaler or the back of a chef's knife, scraping the scales off by moving the knife from the tail end of the salmon toward the head.

substitutions

Salmon has a unique flavor that cannot really be substituted for. With the following recipes, however, you can use another rich, firm-fleshed, meaty fish such as mahimahi, butterfish, or walu.

There are five main varieties of Pacific salmon:

KING OR CHINOOK (*ONCORHYNCHUS TSCHAWYTSCHA*)

The largest species of Pacific salmon (usually weighing from 15 to 35 pounds, although they can exceed 100 pounds) and the least abundant, the king accounts for less than 5 percent of the total Alaskan catch. It is also one of the farthest-ranging types of salmon and is typically caught commercially by hook and line. Unlike other types of salmon, the color of its flesh ranges from white to pink to red. King salmon tends to be one of the fattier types of salmon, making it particularly flavorful and sought-after.

SOCKEYE OR RED OR BLUEBACK (*ONCORHYNCHUS NERKA*)

Unlike king salmon, which feed on insects and small fish, sockeye is a filter feeder (like pink salmon), with plankton its main source of food. *Sockeye* does not refer to any physical characteristics of the fish, but is derived from a Pacific Northwestern Native American word. Sockeye weigh from 8 to 15 pounds at maturity and constitute about one-quarter of the West Coast salmon catch. In the past, sockeye was favored for canning because of its deep red flesh and high fat content, but today an increasing proportion of the catch is frozen and shipped to Japan, where it is particularly prized.

COHO OR SILVER (*ONCORHYNCHUS KISUTCH*)

Coho spends its first year (and sometimes longer) in freshwater and, compared to other types of salmon, the least amount of time at sea, usually returning to its natal freshwater to spawn the following year. When reaching the ocean, coho remains close to the coast and, because it also takes lures easily, is the most important salmon sportfish. Due to significant commercial trolling, its numbers have recently declined dramatically, leading to strict fishing restrictions. Consequently, much of the coho sold is farm-raised. Coho tends to weigh about 10 pounds at maturity and has a lower fat content than other salmon, resulting in a flakier texture and milder flavor when cooked.

PINK OR HUMPBACK (*ONCORHYNCHUS GORBUSHA*)

One of the least far-ranging Pacific salmon, the pink salmon usually remains within a hundred miles or so of the location in which it hatched. It is also the smallest variety of salmon, weighing about 5 pounds when fully grown; however, they account for at least half of the West Coast salmon catch. Much of the catch is canned or frozen, but it is a delicious fish baked whole. As the name suggests, its flesh is pink in color, due to its diet of plankton.

CHUM OR DOG OR KETA (*ONCORHYNCHUS KETA*)

One of the most widely distributed Pacific salmon, chum typically weighs from 10 to 15 pounds at maturity. Historically, it has been the most important type of salmon for coastal Native Americans of the Pacific Northwest. Its low fat content makes it particularly suited to cold smoking, a preserving technique favored in the region for centuries. Chum is typically caught commercially in nets close to river mouths and by trolling, and they are farm-raised in significant numbers. Chum salmon is an underrated variety and one of the least expensive in the marketplace.

Finally, there are two other fish, **cutthroat** and **steelhead** trout, which are now considered to be more closely related to Pacific salmon than to the trout family. They spend between one and three years in freshwater before migrating to the ocean, and unlike salmon, they may spawn several times in their natal freshwater.

pacific salmon recipes

Seared Lemongrass-Crusted Salmon with Watercress-Ginger Sauce | 99

Braised Soy-Glazed Pacific Salmon with Green Tea Somen Noodles and Wasabi-Ponzu Sauce | 101

Parmesan-and-Bacon-Crusted Salmon with Corn, Spinach, and Clam Chowder Sauce | 103

Indonesian Spiced Pacific Salmon with a Sweet and Spicy Coconut Curry Sauce | 105

Twice-Cooked Salmon with Green Tea Risotto and Sour Plum Broth | 106

roy's fish and seafood

seared lemongrass-crusted salmon with watercress-ginger sauce

Serves 4 as a side dish

This intensely green and peppery-flavored sauce, based on French technique, makes a striking visual pairing with the Asian-influenced salmon. The added bonus of this recipe comes from the healthfulness of watercress; my good friend Rafih, who owns Imperial Fez, a Moroccan restaurant in Atlanta, swears by it as the most beneficial food you can eat. You can use swordfish, marlin, mahimahi, or any firm-fleshed fish instead of salmon, if you prefer. This recipe goes very well with steamed jasmine rice or white rice.

Lemongrass Crust and Salmon

- 2 tablespoons minced lemongrass (white part only)
- 1 tablespoon minced garlic
- 1 tablespoon minced fresh ginger
- 1 tablespoon minced shallot
- 1 tablespoon shichimi

Watercress-Ginger Sauce

- 1 bunch watercress, stemmed (reserve 4 sprigs for garnish)
- 1 tablespoon ginger juice (page 231)
- 1 cup warm beurre blanc (page 223)

- 4 salmon steaks, about 7 ounces each
- ¼ cup peanut oil
- 4 teaspoons red pickled ginger

To prepare the crust, combine the lemongrass, garlic, ginger, shallot, and shichimi in a bowl and stir to blend. Set aside.

To prepare the sauce, bring a saucepan of water to a boil, remove from the heat, and blanch the watercress for 15 seconds. Drain thoroughly. Mince the watercress leaves, mix them with the ginger juice, and then stir into the beurre blanc. Set aside and keep warm over tepid water.

Heat a large, heavy dry nonstick sauté pan or skillet over medium-high heat for 2 to 3 minutes. Thoroughly coat one side of each salmon steak with the crust mixture. Coat the crusted side of the salmon with the peanut oil. Carefully transfer to the hot pan, crust side down, and sear for about 1½ minutes, or until the crust is browned. Turn over and sear the other side for about 1 minute longer, or until the salmon is still slightly translucent in the center.

To serve, place a salmon steak, crust side up, in the center of each warm serving plate. Ladle the warm sauce around each steak and garnish with the reserved watercress sprigs and pickled ginger.

braised soy-glazed pacific salmon with green tea somen noodles and wasabi-ponzu sauce

Serves 4 as a main course

Growing up in Japan, I developed a fondness for green tea somen noodles, which typically are eaten cold and sometimes have a little wasabi added to spice them up. In this recipe, I have combined wasabi with a citrusy ponzu sauce instead. Ponzu sauce is typically used as a tangy dip for seafood dishes in Japanese cooking. The cooked salmon can be served warm or cold, depending on the season and your preference.

Wasabi-Ponzu Sauce

- ¾ cup light soy sauce
- 3 tablespoons yuzu juice
- 2 teaspoons freshly squeezed lemon juice
- 1 teaspoon minced fresh ginger
- 1 teaspoon minced fresh shiso
- ¼ teaspoon minced garlic
- Wasabi paste to taste

Pancake Omelet Strips

- 2 large eggs
- 2 tablespoons lobster-dashi stock (page 222) or plain dashi
- 1 teaspoon finely sliced fresh chives
- Salt and freshly ground black pepper
- 1 tablespoon canola oil

Soy-Glazed Salmon

- 1 cup soy sauce
- 1 cup sugar
- 2 scallions (including green parts), sliced
- 1 tablespoon finely grated fresh ginger
- 1 tablespoon minced garlic
- 4 (6-ounce) salmon steaks

Somen Noodle Salad

- 6 ounces dried green tea somen noodles (or plain somen noodles)
- 4 large radicchio leaves
- ½ cup julienned unpeeled Japanese cucumber
- 4 tatsoi leaves

Garnish

- ½ teaspoon diced red pickled ginger
- 2 teaspoons julienned nori
- 2 tablespoons tobiko caviar
- ½ each red, yellow, and green bell pepper, seeded, deribbed, and julienned (optional)

To prepare the sauce, combine the soy sauce, yuzu, lemon juice, ginger, shiso, and garlic in a bowl. Whisk together and then whisk in the wasabi paste. Spoon the sauce into individual ramekins and set aside.

To prepare the pancake strips, whisk the eggs in a bowl and then whisk in the stock and chives. Season with salt and pepper to taste. Heat the canola oil in a continued

continued
from
page 101

nonstick sauté pan or skillet over medium-high heat. Pour in all the batter to form a thin pancake. Cook for about 1 minute on each side, until golden brown. Remove the pancake, julienne, and set aside.

Preheat the broiler. To prepare the soy glaze for the salmon, combine the soy sauce, sugar, scallions, ginger, and garlic in a heavy saucepan and bring to a boil over medium-high heat. Cook to reduce for about 15 minutes, or until syrupy. Place the salmon in an ovenproof dish and brush with the glaze. Broil 5 inches from the heat source, brushing once or twice with the glaze, for about 15 minutes, or until still slightly translucent in the center.

While the salmon is cooking, cook the somen noodles in salted boiling water for 3 to 4 minutes, until cooked through but not soft; drain. Rinse under cold running water to stop the cooking process, and then drain again. Arrange the noodles in each radicchio leaf and place on serving plates. Place the salmon next to the salad and sprinkle with the julienned pancake, the cucumber, and tatsoi. Garnish the noodles with the pickled ginger, nori, caviar, and bell peppers. Place a ramekin of the ponzu sauce on each plate.

parmesan-and-bacon-crusted salmon with corn, spinach, and clam chowder sauce

Serves 4 as a main course

This recipe, from our restaurant in Bonita Springs, on Florida's west coast, was inspired by Jasper White's classic cookbook on New England cooking. I enjoy that style of eating and I love chowders, and these ingredients, which echo traditional New England fare, combine wonderfully well. This dish has proved a huge hit with our restaurant guests, in part because of the unique crust, which can also be used with meatier fish such as tuna and swordfish.

Clam Chowder Sauce

2 tablespoons olive oil

1 tablespoon minced garlic

2 tablespoons minced shallots

1 tablespoon fresh thyme leaves

2 cups bottled clam juice, or 1 cup canned clam juice

½ cup (1 stick) unsalted butter, chopped

Salt and freshly ground black pepper

Corn and Spinach

4 ears sweet corn

Salt and freshly ground black pepper

4 tablespoons unsalted butter

1 tablespoon minced garlic

2 tablespoons fresh thyme leaves

4 cups packed spinach leaves

Parmesan and Bacon Crust

3 slices bacon, cut into ¼-inch strips

8 cloves garlic, minced

1 cup panko (Japanese bread crumbs)

1 cup shaved or grated Parmesan cheese

Salmon

4 (6-ounce) salmon fillets

Salt and freshly ground black pepper

To prepare the sauce, heat the olive oil in a small, heavy saucepan over medium-high heat. Add the garlic, shallots, and thyme, and sauté for about 1 minute. Add the clam juice, bring to a boil, and cook to reduce by half. Gradually whisk in the butter until it is melted and incorporated. Season with salt and pepper to taste. Remove from the heat and set aside.

To prepare the corn and spinach, stand the corn upright on a cutting board and carefully cut the kernels from the cobs with a sharp knife. Transfer to a large, dry skillet and dry roast over medium-high heat for 1 to 2 minutes, until the kernels just

continued

continued
from
page 103

begin to pop. Season with salt and pepper to taste and stir in the butter and gar-lic. Cook until the corn browns slightly, about 2 minutes, and then add the thyme and spinach. Sauté 1 minute longer, until the spinach is just wilted. Set aside and keep warm.

To prepare the crust, put the bacon in a dry, heavy stainless-steel skillet or sauté pan over medium heat and cook for 1 to 2 minutes, or until the bacon is about half cooked and releasing its fat. Add the garlic and continue to sauté until the bacon is cooked but not yet crisp. Stir in the panko and let it toast for about 10 seconds. Add the cheese and cook until melted. Remove from the heat.

Season the salmon with salt and pepper to taste and spread the fillets on one side with a layer of the crust mixture about ⅛ inch thick. Carefully return the salmon, crust side down, to the skillet or pan in which the crust was prepared, and sear over medium-high heat for about 2 minutes, or until the crust browns. Turn over and cook the other side for 4 to 5 minutes, or until still slightly translucent in the center.

Spoon the corn and spinach onto warmed serving plates and smooth out to form a bed for the salmon. Arrange the salmon on top and spoon the warm clam chow-der sauce around the fish.

indonesian spiced pacific salmon with a sweet and spicy coconut curry sauce

Serves 4 as a main course

This recipe, which proves the versatility of salmon, is the product of a week that I spent working in a hotel in Malaysia alongside a chef who cooked in the traditional Indonesian style. I have always enjoyed the curries of the region, and whenever I travel there, I try and taste as many as I can. You can serve this dish with jasmine or basmati rice, and steamed cauliflower, which always goes well with the sweetness of the coconut milk.

Sweet and Spicy Coconut Curry Sauce

1 tablespoon peanut oil

½ tablespoon minced garlic

½ tablespoon minced fresh ginger

10 fresh basil leaves

½ tomato, diced

2 tablespoons fish sauce (preferably nam pla)

2 tablespoons Thai red curry paste

2 tablespoons palm sugar

1 cup canned coconut milk

Salt and freshly ground black pepper

1 cup chicken stock (page 219)

Spiced Salmon

1 tablespoon coriander seeds, crushed

2 tablespoons minced garlic

2 tablespoons minced shallots

1 tablespoon minced fresh ginger

1 tablespoon ground turmeric

1 tablespoon sambal oelek or other chile paste with garlic

4 (7-ounce) salmon fillets

Salt and freshly ground black pepper

¼ cup peanut oil

To prepare the sauce, heat the oil in a heavy saucepan over medium-high heat. Add the garlic and ginger and sauté for 30 seconds, until fragrant. Stir in the basil, tomato, fish sauce, curry paste, palm sugar, and coconut milk. Bring to a simmer, decrease the heat to low, and season with salt and pepper to taste. Cook, stirring occasionally, for about 15 minutes, or until thickened, adding some or all of the stock if the sauce becomes too thick.

To prepare the salmon, combine the coriander, garlic, shallots, ginger, turmeric, and sambal in a bowl and stir to blend. Season the salmon with salt and pepper to taste and coat evenly (on one or both sides, as you prefer) with the crust. Heat the peanut oil in a heavy nonstick sauté pan or skillet over medium-high heat. Add the salmon and sauté for 2 to 3 minutes on each side, or until still slightly translucent in the center. Transfer to warm serving plates and spoon the sauce around the salmon.

twice-cooked salmon with green tea risotto and sour plum broth

Serves 4 as a main course

Ever since I learned to crawl and could lift up a spoon I have enjoyed the traditional Japanese dish of ochazuke: rice soaked in green tea. It is a popular late-night snack (and hangover cure) in Japan. I created this recipe to echo the flavors of that dish; the tartness of the broth gives it a particularly refreshing character. Note that the salmon must first be cured overnight, or for at least 12 hours, before assembling the rest of the dish.

Buy green tea powder in packages at Asian markets. Do not grind up green tea leaves, as the flavor is quite different.

Salmon

1½ cups sugar

½ cup salt

4 (6-ounce) salmon fillets, skin on

½ cup salt

¼ cup wasabi paste

¼ cup olive oil

Sour Plum Broth

2 cups brewed light green tea

2 tablespoons bonito flakes

1 tablespoon dashi

1 tablespoon ume boshi (Japanese plum paste)

Green Tea Risotto

2 tablespoons unsalted butter

2 tablespoons peanut oil

2 shallots, minced

2 cups Japanese short-grain rice

2 cups chicken stock (page 219)

1 tablespoon green tea powder

Salt and freshly ground black pepper

Optional Garnish

2 tablespoons salmon roe

¼ cup daikon sprouts

To prepare the salmon, mix together the sugar and salt and place 1 cup of the mixture in a roasting pan. Score the skin side of the salmon in a crisscross pattern and place the fillets, skin side down, on the sugar mixture in the pan. Sprinkle the remaining sugar mixture over the salmon and then rub in the wasabi paste on the same side. Cover with plastic wrap and refrigerate for at least 12 hours, and preferably overnight.

The next day, preheat the oven to 300°F. Unwrap the salmon and rinse it under cold running water. Pat dry and rub with the olive oil. Place the salmon in a roasting pan and bake for about 20 minutes, until still slightly translucent in the center; check toward the end so that it does not overcook and dry out.

Meanwhile, prepare the broth: Combine all the ingredients in a saucepan. Stir together and bring to a boil over high heat. Decrease the heat to low and simmer for 5 minutes. Remove from the heat and let steep for 10 minutes. Strain the broth into a clean pan. Set aside and keep warm.

To prepare the risotto, melt the butter with the peanut oil in a heavy saucepan over medium-high heat. Add the shallots and sauté for about 1 minute, or until translucent. Add the rice and stir with a wooden spoon for 1 minute to coat. Add the stock, green tea powder, and salt and pepper to taste. Bring to a boil, decrease the heat to medium, and continue stirring until the stock is absorbed and the rice is just al dente, about 20 minutes longer; add a little more stock if necessary.

To serve, spoon the risotto into warmed pasta bowls. Place the salmon on top of the risotto and carefully pour the broth over the salmon. Garnish with the salmon roe and sprouts.

swordfish

shutome or broadbill

(Xiphias gladius)

general description

Swordfish migrate significant distances, making them the most widely distributed billfish in the Pacific; they particularly prefer open ocean waters with contrasting temperatures and currents. Although primarily warm-water fish, they are also found in temperate waters worldwide. Swordfish are typically caught at night by longline commercial fishermen and are most abundant in Hawaiian waters in the spring and early summer; those harvested from this region have a reputation for high quality. Most of the Hawaiian catch is shipped to the mainland. In California, peak season is May through November. Because of its worldwide distribution, swordfish is usually available year-round. In some Pacific Rim countries, gill nets are also used to catch swordfish. Those landed generally range from 50 to 300 pounds in weight, but some may exceed 500 pounds (the larger specimens are female). Like marlin, swordfish were favored by ancient Hawaiians, who fished for them from canoes. Also like marlin, swordfish use their sharp bills (which can measure up to five feet in length, or one-third of the fish's total length) defensively, and were known to pierce the wooden hulls of the canoes. The bills are also used in a slashing motion from side to side to stun prey.

uses, flavor, and cooking qualities

Swordfish is usually sold in steak or loin form (swordfish steaks are distinctive by having four separate symmetrical swirls, or whorls). It has a high oil content, a rich yet delicate flavor, and a firm, meaty texture; the skin is tough and inedible. The color of the flesh ranges from cream to pale pink, but the color does not affect the flavor. Swordfish lends itself to grilling; when cooked, it has a mild, somewhat sweet flavor and a tender, flaky texture. It should be cooked all the way through (unlike tuna), but overcooking will toughen its texture and dry it out. It is favored for sashimi in Japan, and it is increasingly used this way in Hawaii. Like other billfish, swordfish can be successfully grilled and smoked, and it freezes well.

substitutions

There are no close substitutes, although mako shark probably comes closest. However, eating shark meat is regarded as bad luck in Hawaii. Marlin, halibut, tuna, and grouper can also be substituted in most recipes.

swordfish recipes

Soy-and-Butter-Seared Swordfish with Wasabi Ginger
    Butter Sauce | 111

Grilled Garlic Swordfish with Chipotle Chile Sauce and
    Polenta | 112

Broiled Hawaiian Swordfish in Miso with Avocado
    Salsa | 114

soy-and-butter-seared swordfish with wasabi ginger butter sauce

Serves 4 as a main course

I created this recipe in the Japanese *bata yaki* style: cooking with butter. The sauce is a wonderful fusion combination, and the marriage of the spicy wasabi, rich butter, acidic soy sauce, sweet and pungent ginger, and meaty swordfish brings together flavors from all around the Pacific Rim—and beyond—in delightful fashion. You can substitute marlin or tuna for the swordfish with equally tasty results. Serve this dish with rice, if you like.

Wasabi Ginger Butter Sauce

½ cup warm beurre blanc (page 225)

3 tablespoons sake

3 tablespoons mirin

3 tablespoons pink pickled ginger

2 tablespoons minced Maui or other sweet white onion

2 tablespoons wasabi paste

4 scallions (green parts only), sliced

Swordfish

4 (7-ounce) swordfish steaks

2 tablespoons soy sauce

1 tablespoon minced garlic

1 tablespoon minced fresh flat-leaf parsley

3 tablespoons unsalted butter

1 tablespoon diced red pickled ginger, for garnish

To prepare the sauce, put the beurre blanc in a blender. Combine the sake and mirin in a heavy saucepan, add the ginger and onion, and bring to a simmer over medium-high heat. Cook to reduce the liquid until only about 1 tablespoon remains and then transfer the mixture to the blender. Add the wasabi and scallions, purée the mixture, and then strain through a fine-mesh sieve into a clean saucepan. Keep warm over barely simmering water.

Put the swordfish in a shallow bowl or baking dish and coat with the soy sauce, garlic, and parsley. Marinate for 15 minutes in the refrigerator, turning once. Melt the butter in a heavy stainless-steel sauté pan or skillet set over medium-high heat and add the swordfish. Sauté for about 2 minutes on each side, or until just opaque throughout. Transfer the fish to warmed serving plates and pour the warm sauce around the fish. Garnish with diced red pickled ginger.

grilled garlic swordfish with chipotle chile sauce and polenta

Serves 4 as a main course

Here's a recipe with a definite fusion of cultures. Pacific shutome is the tenderest type of swordfish, and I have drawn on Mexican and Italian flavors to create a taste treat. The soft, grainy texture of the polenta contrasts with the meaty fish and thick, smooth sauce, which also makes for a special dish. Chipotle chiles are dried, smoked jalapeños popular in Mexican and Southwestern cuisines, and they are a particular favorite of Jackie Lau, our corporate chef in Hawaii. Jackie has worked with me for many years and draws on her Mexican heritage to great advantage.

Chipotle Sauce

- 1 tablespoon olive oil
- 5 cloves garlic
- 1 yellow onion, diced
- 4 scallions (including green parts), sliced
- 2 tablespoons chopped fresh cilantro
- 6 canned smoked chipotle chiles in adobo sauce
- 1 teaspoon adobo sauce (from the canned chipotles), or to taste
- 1 tomato, diced
- 1½ tablespoons cumin seeds, toasted (see page 228)
- 2 cups chicken stock (page 219)
- 4 cups veal stock (page 220), or 6 cups chicken stock (page 219)

Polenta

- ½ cup (1 stick) unsalted butter
- 2 tablespoons olive oil
- 2 teaspoons minced garlic
- ½ cup finely diced yellow onion
- 1 cup chicken stock (page 219)
- 2 cups milk
- 1 cup fine cornmeal
- 2 teaspoons salt
- ¾ teaspoon freshly ground white pepper
- 6 fresh basil leaves, finely shredded

Swordfish

- 1 tablespoon minced fresh thyme
- 6 fresh basil leaves, finely shredded
- 2 teaspoons minced garlic
- ½ tablespoon freshly ground black pepper
- 1 teaspoon salt
- 2 tablespoons olive oil
- 4 (6-ounce) shutome steaks

Fresh herbs, for garnish

To prepare the sauce, heat the oil in a heavy saucepan over medium-high heat. Add the garlic and onion and sauté until lightly browned, 2 to 3 minutes. Add the scallions, cilantro, chipotles, adobo sauce, tomato, cumin, chicken stock, and veal stock and bring to a boil. Decrease the heat to medium and simmer for about 20 minutes, or until the sauce is thickened; skim occasionally to remove any fat or impurities

continued

continued
from
page 112

that rise to the surface. Remove from the heat and pass through a fine-mesh sieve. Set aside and keep warm.

Prepare a medium-hot fire in a charcoal grill or preheat a gas grill to 450°F.

To prepare the polenta, melt the butter with the oil in a heavy saucepan over medium-high heat. Add the garlic and onion and sauté for 2 minutes. Add the stock and milk and bring almost to a simmer. Gradually stir in the cornmeal and continue to stir for 3 to 4 minutes. Decrease the heat to low and continue to cook for 15 to 20 minutes, or until the polenta is smooth and creamy and no longer grainy in texture; stir occasionally. Season with salt and pepper to taste and stir in the basil.

To prepare the shutome, put the thyme and basil in a bowl and add the garlic, pepper, salt, and olive oil. Mix together well and lightly coat each shutome steak on both sides. Grill for 2 to 3 minutes on each side for medium-rare (depending on thickness), or to the desired doneness. Spoon the warm sauce onto serving plates and place the polenta on the side. Prop the fish up on the polenta at an angle, and garnish with the fresh herbs.

broiled hawaiian swordfish in miso with avocado salsa

Serves 4 as a main course

Of all the swordfish in all the world—and it is found in most oceans—my favorite is Hawaiian shutome, which is superior in both flavor and texture. My favorite cut of the fish is the eye of the loin, which is small in size but deliciously firm and juicy. Marinating the fish for several hours not only enhances its flavor but also helps to keep it moist while cooking. In addition, the acidity of the marinade partially "cooks" the fish, keeping the grilling time to a minimum. This Japanese style of cooking is called *miso yaki.*

Marinade and Swordfish

  ½ cup white miso (shiro miso)

  1½ tablespoons sake

  2 teaspoons firmly packed brown sugar

  ⅔ cup hoisin sauce

  1½ tablespoons minced fresh ginger

  1½ tablespoons minced garlic

  1½ tablespoons freshly squeezed orange juice

  1 tablespoon Sambal Sekera or other chile paste with garlic

  4 (7-ounce) swordfish steaks

Avocado Salsa

2 slices fresh pineapple, peeled and cored, about ½ inch thick

1 ripe avocado, halved, pitted, peeled, and diced

¼ cup diced ripe tomato

2 tablespoons finely diced red onion

½ cup minced scallions (including green parts)

½ jalapeño chile, seeded and minced

¼ Granny Smith apple, peeled, cored, and diced

Juice of 2 limes

½ tablespoon Hawaiian chile water (page 226)

¼ cup chopped fresh cilantro

Salt and freshly ground pepper

1 cup red pickled ginger

3 or 4 unpeeled Japanese cucumbers (about 1 pound), seeded and chopped

Garnish

1 cup canola oil

16 square wonton wrappers, julienned

2 ounces daikon sprouts

1 teaspoon black sesame seeds, toasted (page 228)

1 teaspoon white sesame seeds, toasted (page 228)

To prepare the marinade, combine the miso, sake, sugar, hoisin sauce, ginger, garlic, orange juice, and chile paste in a bowl and stir well to blend. Place the swordfish in a shallow glass or other nonreactive baking dish and pour the marinade over. Refrigerate for 4 hours.

Prepare a medium-hot fire in a charcoal grill or preheat a gas grill to 450°F. For the salsa, grill the pineapple slices for about 2 to 3 minutes, or until browned and caramelized. Dice the pineapple and place in a bowl. Add the avocado, tomato, onion, scallions, jalapeño, apple, lime juice, chile water, cilantro, and salt and pepper to taste. Toss gently to mix thoroughly. Transfer to an airtight container and refrigerate until ready to serve.

Purée the pickled ginger in a food processor until smooth. Strain and set aside. Purée the cucumbers in the food processor until smooth, strain, and set aside.

To prepare the garnish, heat the canola oil in a skillet or wok over medium heat and fry the wonton wrappers for about 30 seconds. Using a slotted spoon, transfer to paper towels to drain. Transfer to a bowl and toss with the daikon sprouts and black and white sesame seeds.

Remove the swordfish from the marinade and grill for 45 seconds to 1 minute on each side for medium-rare, or to the desired doneness. Spoon a circle of puréed cucumber on each serving plate, and then spoon a smaller circle of puréed pickled ginger in the center of the cucumber. Lay a swordfish steak on the puréed ginger and top with a mound of the wonton garnish. Serve the avocado salsa on the side.

tuna

general description

Tuna is an open-ocean fish in the mackerel family that is found in waters around the world; most species have a reputation for migrating great distances. Tuna is an unusual fish, as it is warm-blooded and must swim continuously at a good speed in order to consume enough oxygen. About half of all tuna caught worldwide is landed off Japan and United States, and much of the Hawaiian catch is shipped to Japan for sashimi.

uses, flavor, and cooking qualities

Most tuna is sold in steak form, without the skin, which is tough and inedible. Sashimi-grade tuna is cut from the loin. All types of tuna have a dense, firm, and meaty texture, which becomes flaky and tender when cooked. In its raw state, ahi ranges in color from pink to deep red (larger fish tend to have darker flesh); this rich coloration fades when exposed to the air, and when cooked, the flesh lightens to a light brown color. However, searing or cooking it lightly (to rare or medium-rare) preserves the attractive interior hue. Tuna has a distinctively rich yet mild flavor, and it has a medium-high fat content. Because of its meaty, moist quality, tuna can be successfully smoked or dried, and it freezes well.

substitutions

Most of the tuna recipes that follow can be prepared using other firm-fleshed fish, such as swordfish (Hawaiian shutome), marlin, mahimahi, or opah.

There are several varieties of tuna:

YELLOWFIN OR AHI (*THUNNUS ALBACARES*)

A warm-water fish caught year-round in the Pacific and Atlantic Oceans but more abundant in Hawaiian waters during the summer months, where it is caught commercially by longline boats. Yellowfin in excess of 200 pounds are often landed, although they can reach more than 300 pounds and up to 7 feet in length. The larger, more mature fish tend to have darker flesh and a higher fat content. The texture of the flesh is firmer than that of bigeye (also called ahi in Hawaii), but the two types of tuna are interchangeable in most recipes. Yellowfin is particularly favored for sashimi and poke (the traditional Hawaiian raw-fish salad).

BIGEYE OR AHI (*THUNNUS OBESUS*)

Warm-water fish common to the Pacific, Atlantic, and Indian Oceans. Bigeye is similar in size and appearance to yellowfin tuna (except for the fin length and coloration, and for its unusually large eyes), with which it is interchangeable in all recipes. In Hawaiian waters, bigeye tuna is typically caught in deep water by longline boats; it is more abundant in the winter season, unlike other types of tuna. Bigeye tuna has a higher fat content than yellowfin, which makes it favored by connoisseurs of sashimi and preferred for grilling.

SKIPJACK OR AKU OR BONITO (*KATSUWONUS PELAMIS*)

So-called because this schooling fish often seems to skip across the water. Skipjack is smaller than other types of tuna, averaging 15 to 30 pounds in weight, and is typically caught close to the surface by pole-and-line fishing. The skipjack is distinguishable from other types of tuna by the horizontal stripes along the belly. Historically, this warm-water fish is the most important species in the Hawaii fishing industry and the most common type of tuna landed worldwide (much of the catch is processed for canning). It is more abundant in Hawaiian waters during the summer. Skipjack has a more pronounced flavor than ahi and is preferred by some for sashimi and often used for poke. In dried form (called bonito), it is a popular flavoring in Japanese cooking. (Note: Although skipjack is sometimes called bonito, the Atlantic bonito [*Sarda sarda*] is a different but closely related species and may be substituted in recipes calling for skipjack.)

ALBACORE OR TOMBO (*THUNNUS ALALUNGA*)

Albacore tuna is common in temperate as well as warm water worldwide, and more than with other types of tuna, its availability fluctuates depending on oceanographic and climatic conditions. Albacore is typically caught in deep water by commercial longline boats; peak season occurs during the summer months. Its average weight is 40 to 60 pounds, and it is higher in fat than other types of tuna. Albacore has the palest flesh of all tunas, ranging from off-white to pink. Its mild flavor makes it interchangeable with other types of tuna. Its texture is softer, making it less convenient for slicing into sashimi and more prone to overcooking. Albacore is the only species of tuna that, when canned, may be graded as "white tuna" in the United States.

Other types of tuna, such as blackfin and bluefin, are fished in the Atlantic and Mediterranean rather than the Pacific.

tuna recipes

roy's signature blackened ahi with soy-mustard sauce

Serves 4 as an appetizer

The technique of blackening fish was popularized by Paul Prudhomme in the 1980s, when Cajun cuisine hit the national limelight. This is my Pacific Rim version, and it's been on the menu ever since I opened my first Roy's restaurant in Hawaii in 1988. It's still one of our most popular appetizers, and if imitation is the sincerest form of flattery, then I am most flattered by similar versions you'll find in many restaurants across the States.

Ground sandalwood is the powdered root and wood of a large tree native to Pacific islands and eastern Asia. It is used for both its red color and its aromatic quality for seasoning. It is available in well-stocked Asian markets or direct from Yogi brand in New Orleans, at (504) 486-5538.

Soy-Mustard Sauce

¼ cup mustard powder, preferably Colman's

2 tablespoons hot water

2 tablespoons rice wine vinegar

¼ cup soy sauce

Blackening Spice

1½ tablespoons paprika

½ tablespoon cayenne pepper

½ tablespoon pure chile powder

¼ tablespoon freshly ground white pepper

½ tablespoon ground sandalwood (optional)

8 ounces ahi tuna fillet, about 2 inches thick and 5 inches long

2 tablespoons olive oil

¾ cup warm beurre blanc (page 223)

Garnish

2 to 3 tablespoons pink pickled ginger

½ tablespoon black sesame seeds, toasted (page 228)

1 ounce daikon sprouts

To prepare the soy-mustard sauce, mix the mustard powder and hot water together in a cup to form a paste. Let sit for a few minutes to allow the flavor and heat to develop. Add the vinegar and soy sauce, mix together, and pass through a fine-mesh sieve into a bowl. Cover and refrigerate for at least 1 hour to allow the flavors to develop.

Prepare the beurre blanc and warm in the top of a double boiler.

Mix all of the blackening spice ingredients together on a plate. Dredge the ahi in the spice mixture on all sides. Heat the olive oil in a nonstick skillet over high heat and sear the ahi for 15 to 30 seconds on each side for rare, 1 minute on each side for medium-rare, or to the desired doneness. Remove the ahi and cut into 20 thin slices.

continued

continued
from
page 121 For each serving, arrange 5 slices of ahi in a fan, pinwheel, or cross shape on the plate. Spoon or drizzle a little of the soy-mustard sauce around the tuna, and then spoon or drizzle the beurre blanc around. To garnish, arrange a small mound of the pickled ginger next to the fish and top with the daikon sprouts. Sprinkle the sesame seeds over the soy-mustard sauce.

kalbi korean-style ahi tuna with shiitake-onion-sesame sauce

Serves 4 as a main course

When I travel to Japan, I like to visit some of the excellent Korean restaurants there and sample kalbi, the deservedly famous dish of barbecued marinated beef ribs. The key to good kalbi is the balance of sweetness and garlic in the marinade, and I have added another dimension by spicing up the marinade. Ko chu jang sauce is typically used as a dipping sauce or marinade, and in this recipe you can substitute 6 tablespoons of hoisin sauce mixed with 2 tablespoons of garlic chile sauce. Ahi stands up to these assertive flavors well and, as this recipe proves, is versatile enough to cook in the same style as beef.

Kalbi Marinade and Ahi

- 2 cups soy sauce
- ¾ cup sugar
- ½ cup ko chu jang sauce (Korean chile paste) or sambal sekera
- 6 scallions (green parts only), chopped
- 1 tablespoon chopped fresh ginger
- ½ tablespoon chopped garlic
- ½ teaspoon dark sesame oil
- 4 (6-ounce) ahi tuna steaks

Shiitake-Onion-Sesame Sauce

- ¼ cup unsalted butter
- 1 cup sliced shiitake mushroom caps
- ½ cup sliced Maui or other sweet white onion
- ¼ cup cognac
- 1 cup demi-glace (page 221)
- ½ cup heavy cream
- 1 tablespoon white sesame seeds, toasted (page 228)
- Salt
- 1 teaspoon freshly cracked black pepper

- Salt and freshly ground black pepper
- Steamed rice (page 227), for serving

Prepare a medium-hot fire in a charcoal grill or preheat a gas grill to 450°F.

To prepare the marinade, combine the soy sauce, sugar, and ko chu jang sauce in a bowl and whisk until the sugar dissolves. Add the scallions, ginger, garlic, and sesame oil and stir to combine thoroughly. Place the ahi in a shallow glass baking dish and pour the marinade over. Refrigerate for about 30 minutes.

Meanwhile, prepare the sauce: Melt the butter in a large sauté pan or skillet over medium-high heat. Add the shiitakes and onion and sauté for about 10 minutes, or until the onion is lightly browned. Carefully add the cognac and cook to reduce by half. Add the demi-glace and cream, stir to deglaze the pan, and cook about 3 minutes longer, or until thickened, stirring occasionally. Add the sesame seeds and season with salt to taste and the pepper. Set aside and keep warm.

Remove the ahi from the marinade and season with salt and pepper to taste. Grill for about 1½ minutes on each side for medium-rare, or to the desired doneness. Spoon the sauce onto warmed serving plates, arrange the ahi on top of the sauce, and serve with the rice on the side.

furikake-crusted "rainbow" sashimi

Serves 4 as an appetizer

This is a striking dish: the deep red ahi meat, the creamy white walu, the orange salmon, and the dark green wakame seaweed really catch the eye. This appetizer recipe comes from Greg Ritchie, executive chef and partner at Roy's in Orlando. I tasted Greg's version of sashimi when I was at the restaurant to cook for a wine-pairing dinner, and I enjoyed it so much I asked him to contribute the recipe for this book. Only the freshest fish possible should be used for this dish.

½ cup furikake

5 ounces sashimi-grade ahi tuna, cut into 1 by 3½-inch blocks

5 ounces sashimi-grade walu, pompano, or blue marlin (kajiki), cut into 1 by 3½-inch blocks

5 ounces wild salmon fillet, cut into 1 by 3½-inch blocks

3 ounces wakame seaweed

6 tablespoons soy sauce

3 tablespoons truffle oil

1 tablespoon scallion oil (page 225)

1 ounce ogo seaweed, for garnish

1 tablespoon tobiko caviar, for garnish

Spread the furikake on a plate and roll the ahi, walu, and salmon in it until well coated. Heat a dry stainless-steel sauté pan or skillet over high heat for 2 to 3 minutes or until very hot, and lightly sear the fish for about 10 seconds on each side, keeping it rare. Remove from the pan and cut each block of fish into thin lengthwise slices. Arrange alternating slices of fish in a circular pattern on serving plates and put the wakame in the center.

Pour the soy sauce and truffle oil into a blender and blend until smooth. Drizzle this mixture, and then the scallion oil, around the sashimi. Top each serving with the ogo and tobiko.

kung pao–style spicy ahi tuna with shrimp, mac nuts, and bell peppers

Serves 4 as a main course

Kung pao chicken is a favorite Szechuan dish found on Chinese restaurant menus. I have adapted the recipe to suit the meaty quality of tuna. I have also included macadamia nuts to give it a Hawaiian flair. The kabayaki sauce, traditionally served with eel in Japanese restaurants, gives a pleasing sweetness to the kung pao sauce, while the Indonesian sambal chile sauce provides flavor and heat.

Kung Pao Sauce

¼ cup homemade teriyaki sauce (page 223), or store-bought

2 tablespoons kabayaki sauce

2 tablespoons oyster sauce

2 tablespoons sambal oelek or your favorite hot sauce

Szechuan Vegetables and Shrimp

1 tablespoon dark sesame oil

1 cup julienned red bell pepper

1 cup julienned yellow bell pepper

¾ cup thinly sliced onion

½ tablespoon minced garlic

1 tablespoon minced fresh ginger

2 baby bok choys, quartered lengthwise

4 scallions, cut into 2-inch lengths (including green parts)

12 shrimp (about 12 ounces), peeled and deveined

Tuna

4 (5-ounce) ahi tuna steaks

2 teaspoons sambal oelek

Salt and freshly ground black pepper

¼ cup olive oil

¼ cup macadamia nut halves, toasted (page 228), for garnish

4 cilantro sprigs

Prepare a medium-hot fire in a charcoal grill, or preheat a gas grill to 450°F.

To prepare the sauce, pour the teriyaki into a small bowl and stir in the kabayaki, oyster sauce, and sambal oelek until thoroughly combined. Set aside.

To prepare the vegetables, heat the sesame oil in a wok or skillet over very high heat until almost smoking. Add the red and yellow bell peppers, onion, garlic, ginger, bok choys, and scallions and stir-fry for 30 seconds. Add the shrimp and stir-fry for 30 seconds longer. Add the kung pao sauce and stir to deglaze the pan, then stir-fry until the shrimp is evenly pink, about 1 minute longer.

Season the tuna with the sambal and salt and pepper to taste, and coat with the olive oil. Grill the tuna for about 1½ minutes on each side for medium-rare, or to the desired doneness. Transfer to serving plates and spoon the stir-fried vegetable mixture on top of the tuna. Garnish with the macadamia nuts and cilantro sprigs.

seared black-peppercorn-and-herb-crusted ahi with maui onion–cognac sauce

Serves 4 as a main course

Here's an ahi tuna recipe in the style of pepper steak, proving that ahi can stand up to assertive ingredients just as well as red meat. The Maui onions comple-ment the peppercorns perfectly, a match I began putting together many years ago at L'Ermitage, in Los Angeles. I recommend serving this dish with simple side dishes, such as buttered steamed green beans and mashed potatoes.

Maui Onion–Cognac Sauce

- 4 tablespoons unsalted butter
- 1 cup finely sliced Maui or other sweet white onion
- 1 teaspoon minced garlic
- ¼ cup cognac
- ½ cup heavy cream
- ½ cup demi-glace (page 221)
- Salt and freshly ground black pepper

Black Peppercorn and Herb Crust

- Salt
- 1 tablespoon crushed black peppercorns
- 1 teaspoon minced fresh basil
- 1 teaspoon minced fresh thyme
- ½ cup (1 stick) unsalted butter, softened

4 (7-ounce) ahi tuna steaks

To prepare the sauce, melt the 4 tablespoons butter in a saucepan over medium-high heat. Add the onion and garlic and sauté for about 3 minutes, or until lightly browned. Carefully add the cognac without igniting it and stir to deglaze the pan. Cook until the liquid is reduced by half and then add the cream. Cook to reduce by half again and add the demi-glace. Continue to cook for 3 to 4 minutes, until the sauce coats the back of a spoon. Season with salt and pepper to taste. Set aside and keep warm.

Combine salt and pepper to taste, basil, thyme, and butter in a bowl and stir to blend. Spread one-fourth of the mixture on one side of each tuna steak to coat evenly. Heat a dry stainless-steel sauté pan over medium-high heat for 2 to 3 min-utes. Add the ahi, crust side down. Sauté for about 2 minutes on each side for rare to medium-rare, or to the desired doneness.

Spoon the sauce onto warmed plates and serve the ahi on the sauce.

hawaiian caesar-style ahi poke with avocado toasts

Serves 4 as an appetizer

This appetizer with a distinctively Hawaiian twist has been a standby over the years at Roy's in Honolulu. By popular demand, we still feature it now and again, as a special. Poke is a traditional Hawaiian favorite, and there are countless variations, but typically it is made with cubed raw ahi seasoned with soy sauce, scallions, chopped inamona nuts, and limu (seaweed). Here, I have varied that theme, using some flavorful—and nontraditional—ingredients to give it a Caesar salad–like flair.

Caesar-Style Poke

1 cup canola oil

1 tablespoon drained capers

8 ounces sashimi-grade ahi tuna, finely diced

⅓ cup mayonnaise

1 tablespoon Dijon mustard

1 tablespoon Hawaiian chile water (page 226)

1 tablespoon minced Maui or other sweet white onion

1 tablespoon freshly grated Parmesan cheese

1 teaspoon minced garlic

Salt and freshly ground black pepper

Avocado Toasts

1 baguette, cut into 16 diagonal slices

½ cup olive oil

2 tablespoons minced garlic

1 avocado, halved, pitted, peeled, and cut into 16 thin slices

Preheat the oven to 300°F.

To prepare the poke, heat the oil in a small, heavy saucepan over medium-high heat until 350°F. or a caper sizzles when added to the oil. Add the capers and fry until crisp, 20 to 30 seconds. Remove with a slotted spoon and drain on paper towels. Put the tuna in a bowl and add the mayonnaise, mustard, chile water, onion, cheese, garlic, and capers. Stir to mix thoroughly and season with salt and pepper to taste. Cover and refrigerate.

To prepare the toasts, lay the baguette slices on a work surface. Brush both sides with the olive oil and sprinkle with the garlic. Arrange on 1 or 2 baking sheets and bake until golden brown, about 15 minutes. Remove from the oven and let cool. Place a slice of avocado on each toast and top with the poke. Serve 4 toasts on each plate.

martini of spicy tuna poke with avocado and "inside out" sushi rolls

Serves 4 as an appetizer

This recipe just happens to be made up of ingredients and elements, such as poke and sushi rolls, to which I am particularly partial. It takes the Hawaiian tradition of poke—fresh raw fish that's finely diced and seasoned—and gives it a contemporary presentation in martini glasses. The recipe comes from Roy's in Rancho Mirage, California, where this appetizer dish appears on the menu as a Poke-tini. Likewise, the sushi rolls in this recipe are our modern take on a classic. You will need a sushi mat to make this recipe properly; they are available at Asian markets, kitchenware stores, and some specialty food stores.

Sushi Rolls

1 cup Japanese short-grain rice

1½ cups water

3 tablespoons rice wine vinegar

2 tablespoons sugar

½ tablespoon kosher salt

1 sheet nori

2 tablespoons white sesame seeds, toasted (page 228)

½ avocado, peeled, pitted, and cut into large dice

½ hothouse or Japanese cucumber, peeled and julienned

Salt and freshly ground black pepper

3 fresh shiso leaves

Spicy Tuna Poke

12 ounces center-cut ahi tuna, cut into ½-inch dice

½ cup mayonnaise

4 teaspoons sriracha

1 teaspoon fish sauce

Salt and freshly ground black pepper

Salad Topping

2 ounces micro-greens or chervil

1 tablespoon truffle oil

Juice of 1 lemon

Salt and freshly ground black pepper

½ sheet nori, cut with scissors into 1-inch julienne (7 by 8-inch)

1 avocado, peeled, pitted, and cut into ½-inch dice

Juice of ½ lemon

Salt and freshly ground black pepper

1 tablespoon tobiko caviar

To prepare the sushi rolls, put the rice in a fine-mesh sieve and rinse under cold running water several times until the water draining from the rice runs clear. Drain the rice and transfer to a saucepan. Add the water and bring to a boil. Decrease the heat to low, cover the pan, and let steam for about 20 minutes, or until the rice is tender and the water is absorbed. Transfer the rice to a mixing bowl.

continued

continued
from
page 127

Combine the vinegar, sugar, and salt in another bowl and stir until the sugar and salt are dissolved. Sprinkle the mixture over the hot cooked rice and stir to mix thoroughly. Let cool to room temperature; the rice should appear shiny.

Wrap a sushi mat with plastic wrap so that both sides are covered. Place the nori sheet on one side of the mat and spread the sushi rice evenly on the back of the sheet. Sprinkle the sesame seeds over the rice. Turn the nori over so that the rice is on the plastic wrap. Season the avocado and cucumber with salt and pepper to taste. Layer the avocado, shiso leaves, and cucumber on the bottom quarter of the nori (nearest you). Roll the nori and rice around the vegetables and pull the mat tightly to compress the contents. Continue rolling and pulling until the entire sheet is rolled. Wrap in plastic wrap and set aside at room temperature.

To prepare the poke, put the diced ahi in a bowl, and add the mayonnaise, sriracha, and fish sauce. Season with salt and pepper to taste. Cover and refrigerate.

To prepare the salad topping, toss the greens with the truffle oil, lemon juice, and salt and pepper to taste in another bowl. Sprinkle the nori over the salad mixture.

To assemble the dish, chill four 8-ounce martini glasses. Cut the sushi roll into 8 slices. In a bowl, gently toss the avocado with the lemon juice and salt and pepper to taste. Layer an eighth of the avocado and the tuna poke in each martini glass, starting with the avocado and ending with the poke, and repeat so that each glass has four layers. Garnish with the salad topping and tobiko. Serve each poke martini with 2 slices of sushi roll on a side plate.

vietnamese-style ahi tuna with oyster-lemongrass cream sauce

Serves 4 as a main course

This recipe is a good example of the type of fusion food I enjoy cooking. I have combined elements of Vietnamese cuisine, one of my favorites, with a complementary French-style cream sauce that contains several Asian flavors. One of these is sake, and here, my preference is for my Y brand Wind sake. Chuck Furuya, a well-known sommelier and food expert in Hawaii, and a collaborator on my PBS TV series, describes it as a delicately perfumed, dry, and intense sake with a long finish. Serve this dish with your favorite vegetables and rice.

Marinade

½ cup soy sauce

⅓ cup fish sauce

¼ cup dark sesame oil

¼ cup olive oil

¼ cup freshly squeezed lemon juice

2 lemongrass stalks, minced

2 cloves garlic, minced

6 red Thai chiles, seeded and minced

2½ tablespoons sugar

½ tablespoon freshly ground black pepper

4 (7-ounce) ahi tuna steaks

Oyster-Lemongrass Cream Sauce

1 tablespoon olive oil

½ tablespoon dark sesame oil

2 teaspoons minced garlic

½ tablespoon minced fresh ginger

1 fresh or frozen kaffir lime leaf, minced

2 teaspoons minced lemongrass
   (white part only)

1 teaspoon minced shallot

3 tablespoons dry white wine

3 tablespoons sake

1½ cups heavy cream

2 tablespoons oyster sauce

⅓ teaspoon freshly squeezed lemon juice

½ teaspoon rice wine vinegar

Dash of fish sauce

Salt and freshly ground black pepper

Prepare a medium-hot fire in a charcoal grill or preheat a gas grill to 450°F.

To prepare the marinade, combine all the ingredients in a shallow glass baking dish and stir to mix well. Add the ahi and marinate in the refrigerator for 10 minutes, turning it over once.

Meanwhile, prepare the sauce. Heat the olive oil and sesame oil in a large, heavy sauté pan or skillet over medium-high heat. Add the garlic, ginger, lime leaf, lemongrass, and shallot. Sauté for 1½ minutes, until lightly browned. Add the wine and sake, and stir to deglaze the pan. Continue cooking until the liquid is almost evaporated, then decrease the heat to medium. Add the cream and oyster sauce and bring to a simmer. Cook to reduce the liquid by one-quarter. Add the lemon juice, vinegar, fish sauce, and salt and pepper to taste. Stir well to thoroughly blend and transfer to a blender in batches. Purée until smooth and pass through a fine-mesh sieve into a clean saucepan. Set aside and keep warm.

Remove the ahi from the marinade and grill for about 1½ minutes on each side for medium-rare, or to the desired doneness. Transfer to warmed plates and spoon the sauce around the ahi.

seared soy-marinated ahi with maui onion–fennel salad

Serves 4 as an appetizer

Sometimes I create recipes specifically to combine some of my favorite flavors, and this appetizer is a good example. I really enjoy the aniselike flavor and crisp texture of raw fennel. Together with the sweetness of oranges and the bitterness of radicchio, it makes the perfect partnership with the charred ahi.

Ahi

1 cup homemade teriyaki sauce (page 223), or store-bought

2 (8-ounce) ahi tuna steaks

Maui Onion–Fennel Salad

1 large fennel bulb, trimmed and thinly sliced (about 1 cup)

½ cup thinly sliced Maui or other sweet white onion

2 Kona or navel oranges, peeled and sectioned (page 229)

½ cup shredded radicchio

1 head Belgian endive, thinly sliced

2 tablespoons olive oil

1 tablespoon freshly squeezed lemon juice

Salt and freshly ground black pepper

Prepare a medium-hot fire in a charcoal grill, or preheat a gas grill to 450°F. Pour the teriyaki sauce into a shallow bowl and add the ahi. Marinate in the refrigerator for 10 to 15 minutes, turning once or twice.

To prepare the salad, combine the fennel, onion, orange segments, radicchio, and endive in a bowl. In a separate bowl, combine the oil, lemon juice, and salt and pepper.

Remove the tuna from the marinade and grill for about 1½ minutes on each side for medium-rare, or to the desired doneness. Cut the tuna into slices. Pour the dressing over the salad and toss to combine thoroughly. Arrange the salad on each serving plate and place the tuna slices on top of the salad.

horseradish-crusted ahi with curried lentil mash and saffron broth

Serves 4 as a main course

This is a powerfully flavored dish that brings together the flavors and cuisines of the Pacific Rim, India, and the Middle East. The fresh horseradish gives the ahi some sweet tones and less pungency than prepared horseradish, but if you prefer to accentuate the Asian flavors and increase the spiciness, you can substitute wasabi. There are not many fish that can stand up to such strong flavors, but ahi is one of them.

Saffron Broth

1 tablespoon olive oil

1 clove garlic, minced

1 shallot, minced

¼ cup finely diced celery

¼ cup peeled and finely diced carrot

1 teaspoon minced fresh ginger

1 tablespoon minced lemongrass (white part only)

8 fresh Thai basil leaves, chopped

½ cup dry white wine

Pinch of saffron threads, plus more for garnish

3¼ cups chicken stock (page 219)

1 small Roma tomato, seeded and diced

Curried Lentil Mash

2 tablespoons minced pancetta or bacon

1 teaspoon minced garlic

2 tablespoons minced Maui or other sweet white onion

2 tablespoons peeled and minced carrot

2 tablespoons minced celery

1 fresh or frozen kaffir lime leaf, minced

½ tablespoon Thai red curry paste

1 tablespoon minced lemongrass (white part only)

½ cup brown or green lentils

¼ cup canned coconut milk

2 cups chicken stock (page 219)

1 cup warm mashed potatoes (see page 226)

1 teaspoon minced fresh cilantro

Salt and freshly ground black pepper

Horseradish-Crusted Ahi

5 ounces panko

2 tablespoons grated fresh horseradish

6 fresh basil leaves

1 teaspoon minced fresh thyme

1 teaspoon minced fresh Italian parsley

½ teaspoon minced fresh rosemary

½ tablespoon minced garlic

4 (6-ounce) ahi tuna steaks

¼ cup canola oil

To prepare the broth, heat the olive oil in a small saucepan over medium heat. Add the garlic, shallot, celery, carrot, ginger, lemongrass, and basil and sauté for about 3 minutes. Stir in the white wine. Add the saffron and cook to reduce the liquid until almost dry. Add the chicken stock and tomato and cook to reduce the liquid by half. Strain the mixture into a clean saucepan and add a few more saffron threads for garnish. Set aside keep warm.

To prepare the curried lentil mash, cook the pancetta in a small, heavy saucepan set over medium heat until the fat is rendered, about 2 minutes. Add the garlic, onion, carrot, celery, lime leaf, curry paste, and lemongrass and sauté until the onion is translucent, about 2 minutes. Add the lentils, coconut milk, and chicken stock. Bring to a low simmer, decrease the heat to low, cover, and cook for about 20 minutes, or until tender and the liquid is absorbed. Fold the mixture into the mashed potatoes, stir in the cilantro, and season with salt and pepper to taste. Set aside and keep warm.

To prepare the ahi, combine the panko, horseradish, basil, thyme, parsley, rosemary, and garlic in a food processor and purée. Spread over one side of each ahi steak. Heat the oil in a stainless-steel sauté pan or skillet over medium-high heat until hot and shimmering. Add the ahi, horseradish side down, and sauté for 2 minutes. Using a spatula, carefully turn the ahi over and sauté the other side for 2 minutes longer, until browned on the outside and rare to medium-rare on the inside.

To serve, place the lentil mash in the middle of each warmed plate and arrange each ahi steak on top of the mash. Ladle the broth around the mash.

asian-style tuna melt with avocado and prosciutto

Serves 4 as a main course

A long time ago, before Roy's made it to the drawing board, I worked at a Scandinavian restaurant in Los Angeles where open-face sandwiches were popular. This recipe is my Hawaiian Fusion spin on an open-face sandwich classic. The combination of ahi and prosciutto may seem a little incongruous at first glance, but the ham's saltiness really complements the tuna's meaty flavor as well as the smooth, rich texture of the avocado. Serve with your choice of vegetables and/or rice.

6 tablespoons olive oil

4 (6-ounce) ahi tuna steaks

Salt and freshly ground black pepper

4 cups packed spinach leaves, washed

1 tablespoon minced garlic

2 cups sliced Maui or other sweet white onions

⅓ cup kabayaki sauce

½ cup white miso (shiro miso)

1 cup mayonnaise

2 avocados, halved and pitted

4 ounces prosciutto, finely sliced

4 lemon wedges, for garnish

Heat 2 tablespoons of the olive oil in a heavy sauté pan or skillet over high heat. Season the tuna with salt and pepper and sear for about 30 seconds per side for rare. Set aside.

Heat 2 tablespoons of the olive oil in another sauté pan or skillet over medium-high heat. Add the spinach and garlic and sauté for about 30 seconds. Move the spinach mixture to one side of the pan, tilt the pan, and press out the juices with the back of a large spoon; pour off the juices into the sink. Set the spinach mixture aside.

Preheat the broiler.

In another sauté pan or skillet, heat the remaining 2 tablespoons olive oil over medium-high heat and add the onions. Sauté for about 5 minutes, or until lightly browned. Set aside.

In a bowl, combine the kabayaki, miso, and mayonnaise. Stir to blend and set aside.

Put each seared tuna steak on a baking sheet and spread one-fourth of the spinach and garlic mixture on top of each. Carefully remove each avocado half from the peel with a spoon and cut into 4 fans. For each steak, add a layer of fanned avocado on top of the spinach, a layer of one-fourth of the cooked onions, and then one-fourth of the prosciutto. Cover the top of the prosciutto with the kabayaki mixture and broil 6 inches from the heat source for 5 to 7 minutes, or until the glaze is browned and the tuna is medium-rare.

Transfer the ahi to serving plates and serve with lemon wedges.

aku (skipjack tuna) with wasabi-ogo fusion sauce

Serves 4 as an appetizer

Aku has an even meatier, denser texture than ahi, and a stronger flavor. I enjoy it both raw (as sashimi) and cooked, and this appetizer matches its robust qualities with an equally vigorous sauce based on wasabi. The pungent daikon radish in this recipe and the slightly crunchy ogo seaweed both work to minimize any "fishy" flavor the aku might have. Make sure the kitchen is well ventilated during the searing process.

Wasabi-Ogo Fusion Sauce

2 tablespoons wasabi powder

3 tablespoons water

1 small Maui or other sweet white onion, finely chopped

½ cup finely chopped yellow onion

½ cup finely chopped daikon

¾ cup soy sauce

½ cup rice wine vinegar

Coarsely chopped ogo seaweed

Aku Tuna

4 (3-ounce) aku tuna steaks

1 tablespoon furikake

Salt and freshly ground black pepper

½ tablespoon canola oil

Garnish

2 branches ogo seaweed

1 tablespoon tobiko caviar

To prepare the sauce, put the wasabi in a cup and mix with the water to form a paste. Transfer to a blender and add the Maui onion, yellow onion, daikon, soy sauce, vinegar, and ogo. Purée until smooth and set aside.

Heat a nonstick skillet or sauté pan over medium-high heat for 2 to 3 minutes. Coat both sides of the aku with the furikake and season with salt and pepper to taste. Swirl the oil in the skillet and, when hot and shimmering, add the tuna and sear for about 10 seconds on each side for rare. Remove the tuna from the skillet and thinly slice each steak.

Spoon the sauce onto serving plates and arrange the sliced tuna on the sauce. Divide each branch of ogo in half and garnish each serving. Spoon the tobiko on top. Serve any remaining sauce at the table.

garlic-grilled ahi salad with poached eggs and dijon mustard vinaigrette

Serves 4 as an appetizer

Back in the 1980s, when I worked at Michael's restaurant in Los Angeles, we'd prepare a bistro-style French green salad with frisée lettuce, poached eggs, and a bacon vinaigrette. This recipe echoes that winning combination and also borrows from the unusual pairing of tuna and eggs that forms the foundation of the French classic salade niçoise.

Garlic Ahi

¼ cup olive oil

1 tablespoon minced garlic

1 tablespoon minced fresh tarragon

4 (3½-ounce) ahi tuna steaks

Salt and freshly ground black pepper

Eggs and Pancetta

6 cups chicken stock (page 219)

½ cup rice wine vinegar

Pinch of salt

4 large eggs

½ cup pancetta cut into ½-inch by ¾-inch strips

Vinaigrette

Reserved pancetta fat

2 tablespoons Dijon mustard

¼ cup sherry vinegar

½ tablespoon honey

1 teaspoon whole-grain mustard

½ cup walnut oil

½ cup peanut oil

1 tablespoon minced fresh chives

Salt and freshly ground black pepper

Leaves from 8 heads baby French chicory, or frisée, dark green leaves removed

Prepare a medium-hot fire in a charcoal grill, or preheat a gas grill to 450°F. Combine the oil, garlic, and tarragon in a shallow dish and mix well. Season the tuna with salt and pepper to taste, add to the dish, and marinate in the refrigerator for 10 minutes. Remove the tuna and grill for about 1½ minutes on each side, or until medium-rare. Remove and cut each steak into 4 slices; set aside.

To prepare the eggs, combine the stock, vinegar, and salt in a large saucepan. Bring to a gentle simmer and then carefully crack the eggs into a saucer and slip them into the pan. Poach the eggs for about 5 minutes, or until firm. Remove the eggs with a slotted spoon and set aside. Put the pancetta in a dry sauté pan or skillet and cook over medium heat until crisp, about 2 minutes. Remove the pancetta with a slotted spoon and drain on paper towels; reserve the pancetta fat in the pan.

To prepare the vinaigrette, add the Dijon mustard to the fat in the pan and whisk in the vinegar, honey, mustard, walnut oil, and peanut oil. Add the chives and season with salt and pepper to taste.

Place the chicory on serving plates and sprinkle with the pancetta. Place the sliced tuna on top of the lettuce and arrange a poached egg on top of each serving of tuna. Pour the vinaigrette around the plate and on top of the eggs.

grilled teriyaki-glazed ahi salad with fennel and kona oranges

Serves 4 as an appetizer

Ahi tuna takes well to subtle sweet fruit flavors, and the orangey glaze also complements the refreshing fennel. Kona oranges from the Big Island are particularly sweet, and navel oranges make the best substitutes. Grilling the tuna chars and caramelizes the marinade, bringing out all of its flavor.

Marinade and Tuna

3 tablespoons soy sauce

2 tablespoons olive oil

3 tablespoons sugar

1 teaspoon minced garlic

1 teaspoon minced fresh ginger

½ teaspoon minced scallion

¼ fennel bulb, finely sliced

1 Kona or navel orange, washed and cut into wedges

8 ounces ahi tuna

2 tablespoons canola oil

Walnut-Truffle Vinaigrette

6 tablespoons sherry vinegar

5 tablespoons sugar

1 teaspoon Dijon mustard

¾ teaspoon minced shallot

¼ teaspoon minced fresh flat-leaf parsley

¼ cup walnut oil

1 tablespoon truffle oil

Salt and freshly ground black pepper

Leaves from 2 heads Belgian endive

Leaves from 1 head radicchio

1 ripe avocado, halved and pitted

¾ fennel bulb, trimmed and finely sliced

2 Kona or navel oranges, peeled and sectioned (page 229)

½ cup crumbled feta cheese

Prepare a medium-hot fire in a charcoal grill or preheat a gas grill to 450°F.

To prepare the marinade, combine the soy sauce and olive oil in a shallow bowl and whisk in the sugar, garlic, ginger, and scallion. Add the fennel and orange. Add the tuna and marinate in the refrigerator for about 10 minutes on each side. Remove the tuna from the marinade, pat dry, and coat with the canola oil. Grill for about 1½ minutes per side for medium-rare, or to the desired doneness. When cool enough to handle, slice the tuna and set aside.

To prepare the vinaigrette, combine the vinegar, sugar, mustard, shallot, and parsley in a bowl and whisk in the walnut oil and truffle oil until completely emulsified. Season with salt and pepper to taste and set aside.

Arrange the endive and radicchio leaves in the center of 4 serving plates. Carefully remove the avocado flesh from the peel with a spoon, cut into 4 fans, and arrange next to the endive and radicchio. Place the sliced tuna on top of the greens and drizzle the vinaigrette around. Garnish with the fennel, orange sections, and feta.

seared ahi with lilikoi-shrimp salsa

Serves 4 as a main course

It seems a shame that the bright, vibrant, carmine color of raw tuna turns an indifferent brownish white when it's cooked, but I like to make up for this by serving tuna rare in the center and with colorful accompaniments whenever possible. This delicious salsa is a good example. *Lilikoi* is the Hawaiian word the highly aromatic tropical passion fruit, whose flavor really sets the palate tingling. Here in the islands, the yellow-skinned passion fruit is more common than the purple variety, but you can use either one to equally good effect in this recipe. Serve this dish with rice, if desired.

Lilikoi-Shrimp Salsa

1 ripe passion fruit, halved

4 ounces extra-large shrimp (about 4), peeled, deveined, and diced

½ tablespoon olive oil

¼ cup minced Maui or other sweet white onion

1 large Roma tomato, peeled, seeded, and finely diced (see page 228)

2 tablespoons finely sliced scallion (including green parts)

1 tablespoon minced fresh cilantro

1 teaspoon Tabasco sauce

Salt and freshly ground black pepper

Tuna

4 (7-ounce) ahi tuna steaks

3 tablespoons peanut oil

Salt and freshly ground black pepper

To prepare the salsa, scoop the seeds and pulp from the passion fruit with a spoon and press it through a fine-mesh sieve. Reserve the juice (about 1 tablespoon) and discard the seeds and pulp. Put the shrimp in a small bowl and toss with the olive oil to coat. Set a dry stainless-steel sauté pan over high heat and, when hot, add the shrimp. Sear, turning often, until evenly pink, about 1 minute. Transfer to a nonreactive bowl and add the reserved passion fruit juice, onion, tomato, scallion, cilantro, Tabasco sauce, and salt and pepper to taste. Toss well to combine. Cover and refrigerate.

Put the ahi on a plate, coat with the peanut oil, and season with salt and pepper to taste. Set a dry cast-iron skillet over high heat for 2 to 3 minutes and, when hot, sear the ahi for about 30 seconds on each side for rare, or about 1½ minutes on each side for medium-rare.

Transfer the ahi to serving plates and spoon the salsa over the tuna, letting the juices from the salsa run onto the plates.

uku

gray snapper or jobfish

(Aprion virescens)

general description

Uku, which has a gray body with greenish-yellow markings, prefers shallower reefs than other snappers, ranging between 30 and 300 feet. Most of the catch, landed using both hook-and-line and trolling methods, weighs between 3 and 15 pounds. Unlike other Hawaiian snappers, which tend to be more common in the winter months, uku is landed year-round but is somewhat more abundant in early summer, during the spawning season.

uses, flavor, and cooking qualities

Like other snappers, uku has cream-colored to pale pink flesh that turns white when cooked. Its texture is firm and moist, and it has a tasty flavor that is a little less refined than that of opakapaka, for example. Like other snappers, uku is a versatile fish that can be prepared in similar ways. During the summer months, the flesh is higher in natural fats, making it particularly suitable for sashimi.

substitutions

Other snappers, particularly opakapaka, onaga (long-tailed red snapper), and Atlantic red snapper, as well as sea bass and grouper.

uku recipes

Scallion-Crusted Uku with Char-Grilled
 Pineapple–Macadamia Nut Salsa | 145

Steamed Pesto-Crusted Uku with Watercress Salad and
 a Thai-Style Garlic–Nam Pla Vinaigrette | 146

roy's fish and seafood

scallion-crusted uku with char-grilled pineapple–macadamia nut salsa

Serves 4 as a main course

Crusting fish with scallions and then charring them lightly add another flavor dimension that is familiar to those who enjoy Chinese stir-fry dishes. The tropical salsa features some intriguingly complex flavors and textures: the sweetness of caramelized pineapple, the crispness of jicama and onion, the crunchiness of toasted macadamia nuts, a hint of heat from the chile, the cooling mint, and a dash of pungent fish sauce. Serve this with steamed rice, if desired.

Char-Grilled Pineapple–Macadamia Nut Salsa

- 3 fresh pineapple rings, cored and cut into quarters
- ½ cup peeled and diced jicama
- 1 ripe tomato, seeded and diced
- 2 tablespoons chopped macadamia nuts, toasted (see page 228)
- 2 tablespoons finely diced Maui or other sweet white onion
- 2 tablespoons julienned fresh mint
- 2 tablespoons olive oil
- 1 teaspoon fish sauce
- ½ teaspoon seeded and minced red Thai chile

Scallion-Crusted Uku

- ¼ cup finely julienned scallions (green parts only)
- ¼ cup finely julienned lop chong (Chinese sausage) or bacon
- 4 (7-ounce) uku fillets
- Salt and freshly ground black pepper

Prepare a medium-hot fire in a charcoal grill or preheat a gas grill to 450°F.

To prepare the salsa, grill the pineapple for about 2 minutes on each side, or until caramelized. Transfer to a cutting board and, when cool enough to handle, finely dice. Transfer to a bowl and add the jicama, tomato, macadamia nuts, onion, mint, olive oil, fish sauce, and chile. Mix thoroughly and refrigerate for at least 1 hour to allow the flavors to marry.

To prepare the uku, combine the scallions and lop chong in a shallow bowl. Coat one side of each uku fillet with the mixture and season with salt and pepper to taste. Heat a dry stainless-steel sauté pan over medium-high heat for 2 to 3 minutes. Place the fish in the pan, crust side down, and cook for 2 minutes. Turn and cook 2 minutes longer, or until opaque throughout. Transfer the fish to warmed plates and spoon the salsa over the fish.

steamed pesto-crusted uku with watercress salad and a thai-style garlic–nam pla vinaigrette

Serves 4 as a main course

This dish was inspired by Thai cooking and uses Thai fish sauce. This sauce is a basic ingredient across Southeast Asia, but I prefer the Thai and Filipino versions, which are milder than Vietnamese or Burmese types. The salad and vinaigrette echo the classic Thai green papaya salad. It is important to prepare the salad immediately before serving so the ingredients do not become soggy. Serve this dish with steamed rice, if you like.

Garlic–Nam Pla Vinaigrette

½ cup freshly squeezed lime juice (3 or 4 limes)

¼ cup freshly squeezed lemon juice (1 or 2 lemons)

2 tablespoons sugar

4 cloves garlic, very finely sliced

2 shallots, very finely sliced

1 tablespoon nam pla (Thai fish sauce)

1 tablespoon sambal oelek or your favorite hot sauce

1 tablespoon minced fresh mint

1 tablespoon minced fresh cilantro

Pesto Crust and Uku

2 tablespoons peanut oil

⅓ cup finely sliced scallions (green parts only)

¼ cup fresh cilantro leaves

3 tablespoons oyster sauce

½ tablespoon minced fresh ginger

½ tablespoon minced garlic

Salt and freshly ground black pepper

1 to 2 tablespoons water

4 (7-ounce) uku fillets

Watercress Salad

Juice of 2 limes

1 tablespoon olive oil

1 tablespoon nam pla (Thai fish sauce)

1 tablespoon white balsamic vinegar (optional)

1 bunch watercress, stems trimmed by ½ inch

1 ripe mango, peeled, pitted, and julienned

1 red bell pepper, seeded, deribbed, and julienned

1 yellow bell pepper, seeded, deribbed, and julienned

2 tablespoons roasted peanuts

To prepare the vinaigrette, combine the lime juice and lemon juice in a bowl. Add the sugar and stir until it dissolves. Stir in the garlic, shallots, fish sauce, and sambal. Gently stir in the mint and cilantro. Refrigerate for at least 2 hours to allow the flavors to marry.

To prepare the pesto crust, combine the peanut oil, scallions, cilantro, oyster sauce, ginger, garlic, and salt and pepper to taste in a blender. Add 1 to 2 tablespoons of water and blend to a sauce. Season the uku fillets with salt and pepper to taste on both sides and coat on one side with the cilantro pesto.

Bring 1 inch of water to a boil in a steamer. Place the crusted uku on a rimmed dish or plate that can fit inside the steamer, cover, and steam for 4 to 5 minutes, until opaque throughout.

To prepare the salad, combine the lime juice, olive oil, fish sauce, and vinegar in a bowl. Add the watercress, mango, red and yellow bell pepper, and peanuts and gently toss together.

Place the uku on serving plates and pour the vinaigrette around the fish. Arrange the dressed watercress salad on top of the fish as a garnish.

ulua

jackfish, papio, or giant trevally

(Caranx ignobilis)

general description

A member of the jack family. By definition, ulua weigh over 10 pounds; in Hawaii, smaller specimens are called papio. Typically, ulua are caught up to 50 pounds in Hawaiian waters year-round, although they can grow to well over 100 pounds. Ulua are one of the most prized fish to catch from shore; they prefer deep, rocky water, reefs, and shallow, sandy shorelines, and they are sometimes called "king of the reef fish," as they are major predators of that habitat, along with reef sharks. Some ulua are caught commercially by trolling from boats. There is a traditional Hawaiian saying to describe fierce Hawaiian warriors: *"A'ohe ia e loa'a aku, he ulua kapapa no ka moana"* ("He cannot be caught, for he is an ulua fish of the deep ocean").

uses, flavor, and cooking qualities

Ulua has a rich, buttery texture and a pronounced yet delicate flavor similar to that of butterfish. It is usually available in fillet form, and its texture is dense. Ulua is best sautéed, baked, broiled, or poached, and it can also be dried and smoked.

substitutions

Jackfish, pompano, snapper, and grouper.

ulua recipes

Butter-and-Ginger-Seared Ulua with Minted Passion-Orange Vinaigrette | 151

Dynamite-Crusted Ulua with Avocado, Crab Legs, and Masago Caviar | 152

roy's fish and seafood

butter-and-ginger-seared ulua with minted passion-orange vinaigrette

Serves 4 as a main course

This flavorful, fruity vinaigrette goes wonderfully well with lamb, the dish for which I originally created it. I figured it would make an interesting twist to try it with ulua, and sure enough, it really works well. You could also use tuna for equally successful results. The richness of the butter and pungently spicy quality of the ginger meld perfectly with the sweetness of the vinaigrette, and the beauty of it all is the recipe's simplicity. My favorite side dish with this combination is sweet potatoes; the purple Okinawan variety makes a spectacular presentation.

Minted Passion-Orange Vinaigrette

¼ cup Dijon mustard

¼ cup frozen passion fruit concentrate, thawed

¼ cup frozen orange juice concentrate, thawed

¼ cup rice wine vinegar

½ cup fresh mint leaves

Ulua

6 tablespoons unsalted butter, melted

2 tablespoons minced fresh ginger

2 tablespoons soy sauce

4 (7-ounce) ulua fillets

To prepare the vinaigrette, combine the mustard, passion fruit concentrate, orange juice concentrate, and vinegar in a blender. Add the mint leaves and blend until puréed. Cover and refrigerate.

To prepare the ulua, combine the butter, ginger, and soy sauce in a bowl. Stir to blend. Place the ulua in a shallow dish and pour the marinade over. Refrigerate for 30 minutes. Heat a dry heavy stainless-steel sauté pan or skillet over medium-high heat for 2 to 3 minutes. Remove the ulua from the marinade and sauté for 2 to 3 minutes on each side, until opaque. Transfer to warmed plates and pour the sauce over and around the fish.

dynamite-crusted ulua with avocado, crab legs, and masago caviar

Serves 4 as a main course

This recipe is my tribute to Imanas Tei, a remarkable Japanese restaurant in Honolulu. One evening, I tried their Seafood Dynamite, and it was spectacular. A while later, after I found myself daydreaming about that impressive dish, I decided to try my own version, and after a few twists and additions, this is the result. I'm proud of it, but I can still highly recommend a trip to Imanas Tei so you taste the original.

The orange-colored masago has a very fine texture and is interchangeable with tobiko. It is available from Asian fish markets.

Dynamite Crust

1 tablespoon sesame oil

1 tablespoon minced garlic

4 large spinach leaves, stemmed and julienned

1 teaspoon fish sauce

⅔ cup mayonnaise

3 shiitake mushroom caps, thinly sliced

2 teaspoons rayu (spicy sesame oil)

2 teaspoons furikake

1 teaspoon shichimi

1 teaspoon soy sauce

Salt and freshly ground black pepper

2 tablespoons olive oil

4 (7-ounce) ulua fillets

1 tablespoon masago caviar (smelt roe) or tobiko caviar

1 ripe avocado, halved, pitted, peeled, and cut into 4 fans

4 cooked snow crab or Dungeness crab legs, each about 3 inches long

To prepare the crust, heat the sesame oil in a sauté pan or skillet over medium-high heat. Add the garlic and sauté for about 2 minutes, or until lightly browned. Add the spinach and cook for about 30 seconds, or until just wilted. Stir in the fish sauce. Put the mayonnaise in a bowl and add the sautéed spinach mixture. Add the shiitakes, rayu, furikake, shichimi, soy sauce, and salt and pepper to taste. Stir well until thoroughly combined.

Preheat the broiler. Place 4 scoops of the crust mixture in a baking pan and spread each out with a spatula to the size of an ulua fillet. Broil the crusts 5 to 6 inches from the heat source for about 2 minutes, or until golden brown. Set aside and keep warm.

To prepare the fish and accompaniments, heat the olive oil in a large, heavy sauté pan or skillet over medium-high heat. Sear the ulua for 2 to 3 minutes on each side, or until opaque throughout. Transfer to warmed plates, place a crust on top of each fish, and garnish with the caviar. Arrange a portion of fanned avocado next to (or on top of) the ulua on each plate, and a crab leg on top of the avocado.

seafood

clams

(Mercenaria mercenaria, Mya arenaria, et al.)

general description

Clams, like scallops, are filter-feeding bivalve (hinged-shell) mollusks found in most oceans around the world, and on all the coasts of the United States. There are also some freshwater species. Native Americans used clam shells as "wampum," for trading and ornamental purposes. While most marine clams have hard shells, some varieties (such as steamer or long-neck clams, razor clams, and the giant geoduck clams) have soft shells—actually, thin, fragile shells that do not close tightly due to the "neck," or siphon, that protrudes. Most clams grow on tidal flats or in sandy shallow water, and they are harvested by digging at low tide. Some clams live in deeper waters, and these are dredged. The main edible part of the clam is the adductor muscle that opens and closes the shell, although the "foot" and "neck" of soft-shell clams are also edible. Clams are harvested year-round; on the East Coast they tend to be more plentiful and less expensive during summer months. On the West Coast, clams are more plentiful in winter months.

uses, flavor, and cooking qualities

Clams are usually sold live, in the shell, and should be scrubbed before steaming or cooking. Buy live hard-shell clams that have closed shells; do not buy any that have open or cracked shells. Fresh soft-shell clams will retract their "necks" when touched. All clams bought in the shell should smell fresh and mild. Some types of soft-shell clam, such as steamers or Ipswich clams, tend to contain sand in their shells, so they should be purged by soaking for 2 to 3 hours in a bowl of lightly salted water containing a little cornmeal. Store clams in the refrigerator, covered with a damp towel; do not store in an airtight container or in unsalted water. Clams may also be sold shucked, whole or chopped, or frozen.

If a clam's shell does not open after cooking, discard it, as this means the clam is dead and should not be eaten. Like scallops, clams should not be overcooked, or they will become tough. The flavor and texture depend on each variety, but in general, clams are a little chewy and fairly sweet to the taste. The smaller varieties of clam, such as the East Coast littlenecks and cherrystones, the West-Coast butter clams, and Manila clams (also known as "Japanese littlenecks"), tend to have the best texture and flavor. Larger clams such as quahogs (which are simply large cherrystone and littlenecks, also known as chowder clams) are usually chopped and used for chowders, hashes, stir-fries, and other dishes. The large surf (or skimmer) clams, the most common variety on the East Coast, tend to be less tender and are usually canned. Clams can be eaten raw, but unless you can vouch for the purity of the source, it is not recommended for health reasons, as some clam beds are subject to pollution. Sometimes, clam beds are closed to harvesting by local authorities for this reason.

substitutions

Oysters, mussels, and squid.

clam recipes

clams with wakame and sake

Serves 4 as an appetizer

In Japan, miso soup flavored with dried wakame seaweed is a staple served at any time of the day, for breakfast, lunch, or dinner, together with a main course. Other ingredients are sometimes added, including clams or shrimp, and that traditional combination provided the inspiration for this appetizer recipe. Shungiku, a type of edible chrysanthemum leaf, is used both in its raw form in Japan for salads, and cooked (typically in soups, or pot dishes such as shabu shabu). Available at Japanese or Asian markets, it has a distinctive, slightly bitter taste; if unavailable, substitute mustard greens, turnip greens, or spinach. This dish is always popular whenever we add it to the menu as a special.

¼ cup dried wakame seaweed

2 cups chicken stock (page 219), heated

2 tablespoons peanut oil

1 tablespoon minced garlic

1½ tablespoons minced shallots

24 clams, scrubbed

½ cup sliced linguiça (Portuguese sausage), andouille, or other spicy sausage

6 tablespoons sake

12 shiitake mushroom caps

4 ounces shungiku or mustard greens

2 tablespoons minced fresh flat-leaf parsley

2 tablespoons soy sauce

4 tablespoons unsalted butter

1 package (about 3 ounces) enoki mushrooms, trimmed

In a bowl, combine the wakame and 1 cup of the chicken stock. Let sit for 20 minutes to rehydrate. Heat the peanut oil in a large, heavy saucepan over medium-high heat. Add the garlic and shallots and sauté for 30 seconds, until fragrant. Add the clams and sausage and cook for 1 minute. Add the sake and stir to deglaze the pan. Add the remaining 1 cup stock. Cover the pan and continue to cook for about 3 minutes, or until the clams have opened. Remove the clams with a slotted spoon and set aside; discard any clams that do not open. Add the shiitakes, shungiku, the rehydrated wakame and stock mixture, and the parsley and cook for about 3 minutes longer to heat through. Add the soy sauce and butter, and when the butter is melted, return the clams to the pan.

Arrange 6 clams in each warmed bowl and divide the broth and remaining ingredients evenly among the bowls. Garnish with the enoki mushrooms.

crisp fried ipswich clams with chile and mint

Serves 4 as an appetizer

Ipswich clams are of the soft-shell variety (see page 157) and take their name from the Massachusetts coastal town on Boston's North Shore that was a center of clam harvesting and processing about a hundred years ago. Ipswich clams are the type that New Englanders love to batter and fry, and it's a tradition I have continued with this recipe. I first tried Ipswich clams when acclaimed chef Todd English used them for one of our anniversary dinners, at Roy's in Bonita Springs, Florida. They were so tender, sweet, and flavorful that I decided there and then to create my own recipe with the contrasting flavors of chile and mint, a combination that works very well. This is a great way to begin a meal and to get appetites fired up!

Clams

3 large eggs

1 cup all-purpose flour

2 cups panko (Japanese bread crumbs)

32 clams, preferably Ipswich clams, Manila clams, or littleneck clams, shucked

8 cups canola oil, for deep-frying

2 tablespoons peanut oil

1 teaspoon minced garlic

1 teaspoon minced fresh ginger

1 teaspoon minced red serrano or jalapeño chile (or to taste)

¼ cup julienned red bell pepper

¼ cup julienned yellow bell pepper

¼ cup minced yellow onion

½ teaspoon sugar

1 tablespoon coarsely chopped fresh mint

½ tablespoon minced fresh cilantro

2 teaspoons fish sauce

8 leaves romaine lettuce

8 leaves butter lettuce

To prepare the clams, crack the eggs into a bowl and beat well. Place the flour on one large plate and the panko on another. Dredge the clams first in the flour, then dip into the beaten eggs, and finally, roll in the panko. Heat the canola oil to 375°F in a deep-fryer or deep, heavy saucepan. Add the clams and deep-fry for about

1 minute, or until golden brown. Quickly remove the clams with a wire-mesh scoop or a slotted spoon and drain on paper towels.

While the clams are cooking, heat the peanut oil in a large, heavy nonstick sauté pan or skillet over high heat. Add the garlic, ginger, chile, red and yellow bell pepper, and onion and stir-fry for 2 minutes, until tender. Add the deep-fried clams, sugar, mint, cilantro, and fish sauce and stir to combine thoroughly. To serve, line 4 bowls with 2 each of the romaine and butter lettuce leaves. Evenly divide the clam mixture among the bowls.

crab

(Callinectes sapidus et al.)

general description

Crabs are crustaceans with eight legs and two claws (although some varieties have only six legs). There are thousands of species worldwide, and several types indigenous to the United States are important sources of crabmeat. These include the blue crab (*Callinectes sapidus*), which is native to the Eastern seaboard and Gulf Coast and accounts for half of all crab harvested in the United States; the snow crab (*Chionoecetes oplio* or *C. tanneri*), the king crab (*Paralithodes camtschaticus*), and the Dungeness crab (*Cancer magister*), found in Alaska and the Pacific Northwest; the stone crab (*Menippe mercenaria*), limited mainly to Florida and the Gulf Coast; and the spider or rock crab (*Cancer quanbumi*), also native to the East Coast. Soft-shell crabs, typically harvested from the Chesapeake Bay region, are blue crabs that have just molted; their season is relatively short, from May through August. In terms of size, blue crabs are the smallest (typically weighing up to 8 ounces). Snow, Dungeness, stone, and spider crabs are usually sold in the 2- to 4- pound range, while king crabs can grow up to 20 pounds.

Crabs are caught commercially with crab pots, which are baited wire or metal traps, or as a by-catch of shrimp fishing. With today's refrigeration and transportation techniques, and depending on the season, many crab varieties are available across the country. In Hawaii, Kona crabs are caught around the state, although, as the name suggests, they are particularly abundant on the leeward coast of the Big Island. They are sweeter and more moist than blue crab, although their texture is not as firm. Their peak season is May through August.

uses, flavor, and cooking qualities

Like lobsters, crabs are available live, or cooked and refrigerated, or frozen. If buying them live, choose the most alert ones and avoid any that appear inactive. Store for up to 2 days in the refrigerator, wrapped in damp towels or newspaper. Do not buy or cook whole dead crabs. Cook live crab the same day for peak freshness.

The easiest and most convenient form of purchasing crab is crabmeat, which is usually pasteurized (mostly derived from blue crabs). Although unpasteurized fresh crabmeat is more expensive, it's also the most flavorful form, with sweet, delicate tones, and worth the extra cost. The flavor of fresh crabmeat dwindles the longer you keep it. If you decide to cook crabs yourself for the meat, you should buy five or six times the weight of crabmeat you need in the form of live crabs. Simply boil the crabs in water. The best grade of crabmeat is lump: large sections taken from the body. Flake crabmeat, consisting of smaller pieces, is considered a medium grade, with the browner claw meat less desirable.

substitutions

Lobster, shrimp, and scallops.

crab recipes

kona crab and mango salad with raspberry vinaigrette

Serves 4 as an appetizer

This is another dish that's made for the summer mango season—although these days, mangoes are often available most of the year around. The lush, sweet richness of the mangoes is echoed by the crab, and cut by the tart, flavorful vinaigrette. Although raspberry vinegar was "discovered" by countless chefs in the 1980s, and was rather overdone as a result, it remains a favorite of mine. Fresh crab from Kona, on the leeward coast of the Big Island of Hawaii, is a local specialty that is notably sweet and succulent.

Vinaigrette

- 3 tablespoons olive oil
- 2 tablespoons minced shallots
- 1 teaspoon minced garlic
- 1 teaspoon grated fresh ginger
- 1 teaspoon sliced lemongrass (white part only)
- 1 tablespoon finely sliced fresh Thai basil or regular basil
- 1 cup raspberry vinegar
- 2 tablespoons sugar

Salad

- 1 cup canola oil
- ¼ cup all-purpose flour, for dredging
- 4 ounces firm tofu, cut into blocks about 1½ inches long, ½- inch wide, and ¼- inch deep
- 2 Belgian endives, julienned
- 1 mango, peeled, pitted, and sliced
- 1 fresh heart of palm, julienned, or ½ cup julienned bottled hearts of palm
- 2 cooked artichoke bottoms, cut into ¼-inch slices
- 24 fresh raspberries, for garnish
- 6 ounces fresh lump crabmeat, preferably Kona crab, picked over for shell

To prepare the vinaigrette, heat the olive oil in a heavy sauté pan or skillet over medium heat. Add the shallots, garlic, ginger, and lemongrass and sauté for 2 to 3 minutes, until the shallots turn golden brown. Add the basil and vinegar and remove from the heat. Stir in the sugar until it dissolves. Set aside.

To prepare the salad, heat the canola oil to 375°F in a large, heavy saucepan. Put the flour in a bowl and toss the tofu to coat. Using a long-handled spoon, carefully lower the tofu into the hot oil and cook for about 1 minute, or until golden brown. Remove the tofu with a slotted spoon, drain on paper towels, and let cool.

Put the endives, mango, heart of palm, and artichokes in a bowl and add about ½ cup of the vinaigrette. Gently toss until the salad ingredients are well coated. Transfer to plates and garnish with the raspberries. Arrange the cooked tofu around the salad and top with the crabmeat. Serve the remaining vinaigrette on the side.

roy's crab cakes with lobster cream sauce

Serves 4 as an appetizer

This is one of the first dishes I ever created for the menu at the first, "flagship" Roy's restaurant in Hawaii Kai, in east Honolulu, and it has been a fixture ever since. I wanted a crisp crab cake rather than the heavy, rather soggy version you often find on menus, and the panko crusting makes all the difference. I really enjoy making this lobster sauce, and it forms a great partnership with the crab cakes. Serve this dish with steamed rice or your favorite rice recipe.

Lobster Cream Sauce

2 lobster shells and heads, chopped into quarters

¼ cup olive oil

½ cup chopped yellow onion

½ cup chopped carrot

½ cup chopped celery

2 cloves garlic

2 sprigs basil

1 bay leaf

1 Roma tomato, chopped

¼ cup dry white wine

2 cups water

2 cups heavy cream

Salt and freshly ground white pepper

Crab Cakes

3 tablespoons unsalted butter

½ tablespoon minced garlic

3 tablespoons minced onion

3 tablespoons minced red bell pepper

3 tablespoons minced green bell pepper

3 tablespoons minced celery

3 tablespoons minced carrot

2 tablespoons minced fresh basil

6 tablespoons heavy cream

Salt and freshly ground white pepper

1½ pounds fresh lump crabmeat, preferably Kona crab, picked over for shell

½ cup all-purpose flour

2 cups panko (Japanese bread crumbs)

2 large eggs

1 cup peanut oil

½ each red and green bell pepper, seeded, deribbed, and finely diced

4 strips lemon zest

4 small basil sprigs

Preheat the oven to 350°F. To prepare the sauce, place the lobster shells and heads in a roasting pan and roast in the oven for about 15 minutes, or until orange and slightly browned. Remove and set aside. Heat the olive oil in a large, heavy saucepan over medium-high heat. Add the onion, carrot, and celery and sauté for 2 minutes. Add the garlic, basil, bay leaf, tomato, and roasted lobster heads. Add the white wine, stir to deglaze the pan, and cook for 1 minute. Add the water, bring

continued

continued
from
page 166

to a simmer, and decrease the heat to low. Cook at a low simmer for 15 minutes. Increase the heat to high and cook to reduce the liquid by three-quarters. Add the cream and cook 10 minutes longer, until slightly thick. Remove the pan from the heat and strain the liquid into a clean saucepan, pressing down on the solids with a wooden spoon to extract as much of the liquid as possible. Set over medium heat and cook for about 10 minutes, or until the sauce is thick enough to coat the back of a spoon. Season with salt and pepper to taste. Remove from the heat and let cool. Cover and refrigerate.

While the sauce is cooking, prepare the crab cakes. Melt the butter in a large sauté pan or skillet over medium-high heat. Add the garlic and onion and sauté for about 1 minute, or until golden brown. Add the red and green bell pepper, celery, carrot, and basil and sauté 1 minute longer. Add the cream and continue cooking until the liquid is reduced by half. Season with salt and pepper to taste and transfer to a nonreactive bowl. Let cool. Cover and refrigerate for 1 hour.

Add the crabmeat to the chilled mixture and stir thoroughly. Form into 8 balls and squeeze gently to remove any excess liquid; then form the balls into patties. Place the flour and panko on separate plates and beat the eggs in a shallow bowl. Lightly coat the crab cakes in the flour, then in the egg, and finally, in the panko. Heat the peanut oil in a heavy sauté pan or skillet over medium heat until it reaches 350°F. Add the crab cakes and sauté for about 1 1/2 minutes on each side, or until evenly browned.

Warm the sauce over low heat and ladle onto serving plates. Serve 2 crab cakes per person. Garnish with the red and green bell pepper and lemon zest. Top with a basil sprig.

truffled crab chawan moshi

Serves 4 as an appetizer

In traditional Japanese cuisine, this steamed ("moshi") dish is served in a teacup-like container with a lid and consists of morsels of chicken, shrimp, ginkgo nut, and mitsuba, an edible flower. This is my updated version, and I have added two of my favorite ingredients: truffles and crab. I like to put this dish on the menu whenever we open a new restaurant, and it's popular for private parties.

Savory Custard

    3 large eggs
    3 cups lobster-dashi stock (page 222)
    ¼ cup sake
    1 teaspoon light soy sauce
    1 teaspoon salt
    ½ teaspoon sugar

Crab Topping

    6 ounces fresh lump crabmeat, preferably Kona crab, picked over for shell
    2 tablespoons white truffle oil
    Juice of 1 lemon
    ½ tablespoon soy sauce

Garnish

    2 tablespoons minced fresh chervil
    1 tablespoon tobiko caviar

To prepare the custard, break the eggs into a bowl and use chopsticks to lift up the egg whites 3 or 4 times; this mixes the eggs without beating air into them. Add the lobster-dashi stock, sake, soy sauce, salt, and sugar. Mix well with the chopsticks and strain through a fine-mesh sieve into a clean bowl. Bring 1 to 2 inches of water to a boil in a steamer. Pour the custard mixture into four 5-ounce ramekins or serving bowls and place on the steaming rack. Cover and steam for about 8 minutes. The custard will bubble and separate; when it jiggles slightly, it is done.

While the custard is cooking, prepare the crab topping. Combine the crabmeat, truffle oil, lemon juice, and soy sauce in a bowl and mix thoroughly. Remove the custards from the steamer and top each serving with the crab mixture. Garnish with the chervil and tobiko.

crab ravioli in a red wine crab sauce

Serves 4

Every August, an international wine festival is held in McMinnville, Oregon, north of Salem, to celebrate Pinot Noir. This is entirely appropriate, as the surrounding area produces some consistently excellent vintages. One year, as a guest chef at the festival, I created this appetizer to feature—and to match—a particular Pinot, and we have often served this dish at Roy's since then. The red wine sauce is highly versatile, and can be paired just as well with lobster, most fish, and even chicken. Homemade ravioli make an elegant presentation, and are fun to make.

Gyoza wrappers are made with flour and water; Chinese wontons are made with flour, water, and egg.

Red Wine Crab Sauce

⅓ cup demi-glace (page 221)

¼ cup Pinot Noir wine

3 tablespoons unsalted butter

4 ounces fresh lump crabmeat, preferably Kona crab, picked over for shell

1 tablespoon finely sliced fresh chives

Ravioli

½ tablespoon peanut oil

1 teaspoon minced garlic

1 teaspoon minced fresh ginger

2 scallions (including green parts), minced

2 tablespoons minced shiitake mushroom caps

8 ounces extra-large shrimp (about 8), peeled and deveined

1 teaspoon minced fresh mint

2 teaspoons minced fresh cilantro

3 ounces crabmeat, preferably Kona crab, picked over for shell

1 teaspoon fish sauce

Pinch of freshly ground black pepper

8 gyoza wrappers or round wonton wrappers

1 large egg yolk, beaten

Garnish

4 sprigs (2 inches long) chervil or flat-leaf parsley

1 teaspoon tobiko caviar

To prepare the sauce, combine the demi-glace and wine in a heavy saucepan. Bring to a boil over medium-high heat, decrease the heat to medium-low, and cook to reduce until the sauce is thick enough to coat the back of a spoon. Swirl in the butter and stir in the crabmeat and chives. Remove from the heat and let cool. Cover and refrigerate.

To prepare the ravioli, heat the oil in a sauté pan or skillet over medium-high heat. Add the garlic and ginger and sauté for 2 to 3 minutes, until the mixture just begins to turn golden brown. Add the scallions, mushrooms, mint, and cilantro, and cook for 1 minute. Remove from the heat and let cool. Grind half of the shrimp using a grinder with large-hole attachment or blend in a blender and add to the mixture. Coarsely chop the remaining half of the shrimp and add to the mixture. Fold in the crabmeat, fish sauce, and pepper.

Place a gyoza wrapper on a work surface and place about 1 1/2 tablespoons of the filling in the center of the wrapper. Brush the edge of the wrapper with the beaten egg yolk and place another wrapper over the mixture. Press the edges together to seal. Repeat with the remaining wrappers and filling. In a large pot of salted boiling water, cook the ravioli for about 2 minutes, or until they have risen to the surface of the water. Drain.

Reheat the sauce over low heat. Arrange the ravioli on warmed plates. Pour the sauce over the ravioli and garnish with the chervil and tobiko.

lobster

(Homarus americanus)

general description

The American or northern (or "Maine") lobster is a close relation of the European lobster (*Homarus gammarus*). The North American crustaceans typically weigh between 1 and 2 pounds, and according to state and federal regulations, must measure at least 3 1/4 inches long from eye socket to the beginning of the tail to be legally harvested (this convention was introduced to protect the stock of lobsters). American lobsters are native to Atlantic coastal waters, from Canada south to the Carolinas. It is hard to imagine that in colonial times, lobster (like oysters) was so plentiful that it was looked down upon as a second-class food that only the poor would eat. During the nineteenth century, stocks declined, tastes changed, and following European habits, lobster became a luxury item.

There are also several types of spiny lobster (such as *Palinurus argus,* or *P. mauritanicus*) and rock lobster (such as *Jasus edwardsii*), which do not have claws; they are most commonly categorized by whether they are harvested from warm or cold waters. Some prefer the quality and texture of cold-water spiny lobster (from New Zealand and Australia, for example) to that of warm-water lobsters (from Florida, California, the Caribbean, and tropical South America). My personal preference is to cook with our local Hawaiian spiny lobster, or the spiny lobster from Japan.

Lobster is generally available in two forms: live and frozen lobster tails. Live (American) lobsters, which are most often dark green or dark blue to black in color, are usually held in tanks or on ice. When buying them, check that they appear lively (make sure their claws are secured by a band before handling). If possible, buy from a source with high turnover. If you are not cooking the lobster immediately, store it for a day or two in the refrigerator, wrapped in damp newspaper. Frozen lobster tails are usually taken from spiny lobsters.

uses, flavor, and cooking qualities

The richness and natural flavor of lobster make it one type of seafood that can be eaten with no embellishment, or with the simplest of accompaniments, such as clarified butter or fresh lemon. It takes about five 1-pound lobsters to yield 1 pound of cooked lobster meat.

For live lobsters, there are two schools of thought regarding the best—and most humane—method of killing them. The first is to plunge them headfirst into a large saucepan or stockpot of boiling water and cook until limp or completely done. The second technique is to plunge a sharp chef's knife into the lobster's head, just behind the eyes, to kill it by severing the spinal cord. The lobster can then be steamed, broiled, grilled, baked, or sautéed.

substitutions

Shrimp, crab, clams, and mussels.

lobster recipes

buttered garlic-style chinese lobster

Serves 4 as a main course

Few foods seem as indulgent—or as rich—as lobster paired with butter, especially a good-quality butter that has been clarified so the milk solids are drawn off. It's a simple but classic combination that the chefs at my former restaurant in Hong Kong refined and then improved upon with this dish. Serve this dish with rice and green beans or Japanese eggplant, if desired.

1 cup cornstarch, plus 3 tablespoons

Salt and freshly ground black pepper

3 tablespoons water

3½ cups canola oil

¾ cup dark sesame oil

4 live lobsters, about 1 ½ pounds each

¼ cup light sesame oil

¼ cup minced garlic

2 shallots, minced

1 tablespoon minced fresh ginger

¾ cup chicken stock (page 219), strained through cheesecloth

2 tablespoons chopped fresh cilantro

⅓ cup clarified unsalted butter (page 229), at room temperature

Place the 1 cup cornstarch on a plate and season with salt and pepper to taste. In a small bowl, mix the 3 tablespoons of cornstarch with the water to form a paste and set aside. Add the canola oil and dark sesame oil to a deep fryer or a large, heavy saucepan and heat to 375°F.

To cut the lobsters in half, place each one on its stomach (right side up) and plunge a sharp chef's knife about an inch behind the eyes. Cut in half lengthwise. Remove the claws from the body and lightly crack them. Coat the lobster halves with the seasoned cornstarch and add to the hot oil. Cook for about 2 minutes, or until cooked about three-quarters of the way through. Remove with tongs and drain on paper towels.

Heat the light sesame oil into a wok or large, heavy skillet (big enough to hold the lobsters) over high heat until hot and shimmering. Add the garlic, shallots, and ginger and stir-fry for 30 seconds to 1 minute, until the shallots are translucent. Add the cooked lobster halves and the stock and cook for 1 minute. Pour the reserved cornstarch paste mixture into the wok and add 1 tablespoon of the cilantro and the butter. Stir until the butter is melted and the mixture is thickened.

Transfer each lobster half and the butter mixture to warmed plates and garnish with the remaining cilantro.

grilled spiny lobster with bean thread noodles and macadamia nuts

Serves 4 as an appetizer

Warm-water spiny lobsters are smaller and sweeter than Maine lobsters, and most lobster tails you see marketed come from spiny lobsters. Spiny lobsters are also easier to eat, because there is no claw meat to negotiate. Bean thread noodles are usually sold in the Asian section of supermarkets, or in Asian food markets, and may also be labeled cellophane noodles, saifun, or vermicelli.

2 spiny lobster tails, 7 to 8 ounces each

2 tablespoons peanut oil

6 to 8 ounces bean thread noodles

Ginger-Scallion Sauce

1 teaspoon dark sesame oil

½ cup finely diagonally sliced scallions (including green parts)

⅓ cup soy sauce

1½ tablespoons sugar

½ tablespoon grated fresh ginger

1 teaspoon minced garlic

Garnish

1 teaspoon canola oil

2 tablespoons julienned red bell pepper

2 tablespoons julienned green bell pepper

2 tablespoons julienned yellow bell pepper

1 teaspoon black sesame seeds, toasted (page 228)

1 teaspoon white sesame seeds, toasted (page 228)

2 tablespoons crushed macadamia nuts, toasted (page 228)

2 teaspoons furikake (optional)

4 sprigs cilantro

Prepare a hot fire in a charcoal grill or preheat a gas grill to medium-high. Brush the lobster tails on both sides with the peanut oil and grill flat side down for about 5 minutes, or until opaque throughout. Remove from the grill, and when cool enough to handle, remove the meat from the shells, dice it, and set aside.

Cook the noodles in a large pot of boiling water for 5 minutes, or until tender. Drain in a sieve, rinse under cold running water, drain again, and set aside.

To prepare the sauce, heat the sesame oil in a heavy saucepan over high heat until hot and shimmering. Add the scallions and sauté for 10 to 15 seconds. Stir in the soy sauce, sugar, ginger, and garlic. Immediately remove from the heat and set aside.

To prepare the garnish, heat the canola oil in a large nonstick sauté pan or skillet over medium-high heat until almost smoking. Add the red, green, and yellow bell pepper and sauté for 30 seconds, until softened. Set aside.

continued

continued
from
page 177

Transfer the cooked noodles to the saucepan containing the sauce and cook over low heat until the noodles have completely absorbed the sauce. Add the diced lobster and remove from the heat. Transfer to warmed serving plates and garnish with the bell peppers, sesame seeds, and macadamia nuts. Sprinkle the furikake on top of the lobster and garnish with the cilantro sprigs.

lobster with garlic–black bean sauce and crisp pan-fried egg noodle cakes

Serves 4 as an appetizer

This recipe is based on a classic Chinese dish of crab with black bean sauce and pan-fried noodles. I first cooked a version of this dish—using mussels as the main ingredient—for a garlic festival we held at 385 North, my restaurant in Los Angeles that preceded the very first Roy's restaurant in Honolulu. You can also use shrimp, chicken, or clams in this recipe instead of the lobster, if you prefer.

Crisp Pan-Fried Egg Noodle Cakes

1 package (16 ounces) fresh thin Chinese egg noodles

1 bunch cilantro, stemmed and minced

4 scallions (including green parts), minced

1 tablespoon minced garlic

4 tablespoons sesame oil

Salt and freshly ground black pepper

1 (2 pound) lobster

3 tablespoons sesame oil

1 tablespoon minced garlic

1 teaspoon minced fresh ginger

1 small red bell pepper, seeded, deribbed, and julienned

1 small yellow bell pepper, seeded, deribbed, and julienned

1 piece lop chong (Chinese sausage) or sweet Italian sausage, cut into thin diagonal slices

⅓ cup fermented black beans, rinsed, drained, and coarsely chopped

¼ cup dry sherry

1 cup lobster-dashi stock (page 222)

5 tablespoons sugar

¼ cup oyster sauce

1 tablespoon soy sauce

2 tablespoons cornstarch

2 tablespoons water

1 tablespoon minced fresh chives

To prepare the egg noodle cakes, combine the noodles, cilantro, scallions, garlic, and 1 tablespoon of the sesame oil in a bowl and mix thoroughly; season with salt and pepper to taste. Heat the remaining 3 tablespoons oil in a large, heavy sauté pan or skillet over medium-low heat until fragrant. Use tongs to transfer one-quarter of the noodle mixture to the pan and shape into a round cake. Cook for 3 to 4 minutes, or until the bottom of the cake is crisp. Carefully flip over with a spatula and cook 3 to 4 minutes longer, or until crisp. Remove from the pan, drain on paper towels, and keep warm. Repeat with the remaining noodle mixture.

To prepare the lobster, fill a large stock pot with water and bring to a boil. Completely submerge the lobster into the boiling water, turn off the heat, and allow it to sit in the pot for 12 minutes. Remover the lobster from the pot and allow it to cool for 30 minutes at room temperature. When cool, hold the head in one hand and the body in the other hand and twist to separate. Using kitchen scissors, cut the underside from top to bottom and pull out the meat. Cut all of the meat into ¹/₂ inch cubes.

To finish the dish, heat the 3 tablespoons sesame oil in a large, heavy sauté pan or skillet over medium-high heat. Add the garlic, ginger, red and yellow bell pepper, lop chong, and black beans and sauté for 2 to 3 minutes, until the bell peppers are soft. Add the sherry, stir to deglaze the pan, and cook for 30 seconds. Add the lobster stock and lobster meat and stir until completely incorporated and heated through. Stir in the sugar, oyster sauce, and soy sauce. In a cup, mix the cornstarch and water to form a paste and add to the pan slowly, while stirring. When the mixture thickens enough to coat the back of a spoon, cook 1 minute longer.

Place the cooked noodles on warmed plates and spoon the lobster mixture on top. Garnish with the chives.

mussels

(Mytilus edulis et al.)

general description

Like scallops and clams, mussels are filter-feeding bivalve (hinged-shell) mollusks. There are many varieties worldwide, and the most common in U.S. waters is the blue or common mussel (sometimes also referred to as the black mussel), measuring 2 to 3 inches in length on average. This mussel is found on both the Eastern seaboard and the West Coast, and gets its name from the blue-black shell. Another popular mussel is the green-lipped variety from New Zealand (*Perna canaliculus*). Mussels grow in clusters on rocks or piers or other marine structures (as well as on boat hulls), attached by byssal threads (the mussel's "beard"), and they are also cultivated on long ropes suspended from rafts moored on the surface. Most mussels harvested commercially in the United States are cultivated, and have the advantage of not containing sand or grit. The edible part of the mussel is the adductor muscle that opens and closes the shell. Mussels are harvested year-round, although on the West Coast they are in season during the winter months.

uses, flavor, and cooking qualities

Mussels have been eaten by coastal dwellers around the world for thousands of years. Usually sold live, in the shell, they should be scrubbed and debearded before steaming or cooking. Avoid overly muddy mussels. Buy live mussels that have closed shells or that close when touched; do not buy any that remain open or that have cracked shells. Mussels bought in the shell should smell fresh and mild. Store mussels in the refrigerator, covered with a damp towel, and do not keep in an airtight container or in unsalted water. Mussels may also be sold shucked, whole or chopped, or frozen.

    Once cooked, if the shell of the mussel does not open, discard the mussel as this means it is dead and should not be eaten. The meat of mussels is a little less chewy than that of clams, and the flavor is quite sweet and delicious. Like scallops and clams, mussels can be eaten raw, but for health reasons, this is not recommended. When cooking them, do not overcook or they will become tough.

substitutions

Clams and oysters.

mussel recipes

oven-roasted mussels with hawaiian chile water and butter

Serves 4 as an appetizer

For simple steamed mussels with a Hawaiian Fusion twist, look no further than this recipe. I often barbecue for friends and family on holidays such as July Fourth and Labor Day, and if I'm preparing clams, oysters, mussels, or opihi on the grill, I have always sprinkled a little chile water over the seafood first to give it a little "oomph." Recently, when I was looking to add a seafood appetizer at the restaurant, I decided to let my guests try this taste of home cooking, and it proved a popular choice. It's an appetizer that cries out to be enjoyed with your favorite beer.

Garlic-Parsley Butter

¾ cup (1½ sticks) unsalted butter, softened

1 teaspoon minced garlic

¼ cup minced fresh flat-leaf parsley

40 mussels, scrubbed and debearded

2 tablespoons Hawaiian chile water (page 226)

¼ cup soy sauce

Juice of 1 lime

Preheat the broiler. To prepare the butter, combine the butter, garlic, and parsley in a bowl and stir to blend well. Set aside.

Heat a dry cast-iron skillet under the broiler for about 5 minutes until it becomes very hot. Using oven mitts, remove the skillet and add the mussels. Dollop half of the prepared butter over the mussels and place the skillet under the broiler again, 5 to 6 inches from the heat source. Cook for 5 to 6 minutes, until the mussels have opened; discard any that do not open. Pour the chile water and soy sauce over the mussels, stir to deglaze the pan, and add the remaining butter. Transfer the mussels to warmed serving bowls, pour the sauce from the pan over the mussels, and spritz some lime juice over the top.

iron-skillet mussels with coconut-carrot sauce

Serves 4

The more toys you have in the kitchen, the easier it is, sometimes, to get those creative juices flowing. At Roy's, our wood-fired brick pizza oven is an integral feature of the kitchen—after all, we use it constantly during our dinner service for our highly popular line of Hawaiian Fusion pizzas. I felt it was time to make use of our oven and our cast-iron skillets, using a technique similar to Mongolian barbecue, to put some sizzle into this mussel dish. On the off chance that you do not happen to have a pizza oven in your home, your broiler will work just as effectively. In this recipe, carrot juice and coconut milk may seem like an unlikely combination, but their flavors and subtle sweetness go very well together. If you'd like the sauce a little spicier, use rayu—Japanese sesame-chile oil—instead of peanut oil to sauté the ingredients.

Coconut-Curry Sauce

2 cups chicken stock (page 219)

2 tablespoons peanut oil

1 tablespoon minced garlic

2 tablespoons minced fresh ginger

1 cup canned coconut milk

1 cup carrot juice

10 fresh basil leaves

5 fresh or frozen kaffir lime leaves

1 tablespoon palm sugar or granulated sugar

Salt and freshly ground black pepper

Mussels

40 mussels, scrubbed and debearded

1 bulb roasted garlic (page 228), broken up into individual cloves

2 tablespoons finely julienned fresh ginger

Juice of 1 lime

Salt and freshly cracked black pepper

Garnish

1 small carrot, peeled and thinly sliced

½ sliced celery stalk, thinly slivered

To prepare the sauce, bring the stock to a boil in a saucepan over high heat. Continue to cook to reduce until 1 cup remains. Meanwhile, heat the peanut oil in a heavy saucepan over medium-high heat. Add the garlic and ginger and sauté for 1 minute. Add the coconut milk, carrot juice, reduced stock, basil, lime leaves, and palm sugar and bring to a simmer. Decrease the heat to medium-low and simmer for 8 to 10 minutes, until the sauce thickens enough to coat the back of a spoon. Strain into a clean saucepan and season with salt and pepper to taste. Set aside and keep warm.

Preheat the broiler. Place a dry, heavy cast-iron skillet under the broiler for about 5 minutes, or until it becomes very hot. Very carefully add the mussels, roasted garlic cloves, and ginger to the skillet. Drizzle with lime juice, sprinkle with salt and

continued

continued
from
page 184

pepper to taste, and return to the broiler, about 5 to 6 inches from the heat source, for about 5 minutes, or until the mussels have opened. Discard any mussels that do not open. Transfer the mussels to warmed bowls and spoon the sauce over. Garnish with the slivered carrot and celery.

mussels with rice noodles and red curry sauce

Serves 4 as an appetizer

This Thai-inspired dish combines several ingredients I most enjoy eating: shellfish, curry sauce, and rice noodles. The flat pad thai noodles are available at specialty Asian stores, or you can substitute regular white rice noodles. Most Asian noodle dishes involve stir-frying, but this one is an exception. You can substitute clams, calamari, or chicken for the mussels, and you can prepare the dish as a bed for a fish main course—shutome (swordfish) would be an excellent choice.

8 ounces dried pad thai rice noodles

¼ cup dark sesame oil

2 tablespoons minced garlic

2 tablespoons grated fresh ginger

32 mussels, scrubbed and debearded

¾ cup sake

1 cup chicken stock (page 219)

Juice of 1 lemon (optional)

1 small carrot, peeled and julienned

1 red bell pepper, seeded, deribbed, and julienned

1 yellow bell pepper, seeded, deribbed, and julienned

2 baby bok choy, quartered lengthwise

20 fresh basil leaves

3 tablespoons chopped fresh cilantro

4 fresh or frozen kaffir lime leaves, thinly sliced

2 tablespoons red Thai curry paste, or to taste

1 can (19 ounces) coconut milk

½ cup fish sauce

Salt and freshly ground black pepper

Put the rice noodles in a bowl of cold water and soak for 1 hour.

Heat the sesame oil in a large saucepan over medium-high heat until almost smoking. Add the garlic, ginger, and mussels and sauté for 1½ minutes, until fragrant. Add the sake and stir to deglaze the pan. Add the stock, cover the pan, and bring to a boil. Cook for 1¹/₂ minutes longer, until the mussels open. Remove the mussels with a slotted spoon and set aside; discard any mussels that do not open. Add the lemon juice, carrot, red and yellow bell pepper, bok choy, basil, cilantro, lime leaves, curry paste, and coconut milk. Stir well, bring to a boil, and cook for 5 minutes, until the vegetables are tender. Add the fish sauce and season with salt and pepper to taste. Return the mussels to the pan and reheat for 30 seconds. Drain the noodles and divide among warmed bowls. Divide the mussels and sauce among the bowls, on top of the rice noodles.

opihi

(Cellana exarata)

general description

Opihi is the local name for the Hawaiian limpet, which is found only in the Hawaiian Islands, on volcanic (basalt) shorelines. All limpets are snails in the gastropod family that are common to rocky coasts worldwide. Their shells measure 1 to 2 inches across, are gray and black, and are shaped like Chinese "coolie" straw hats. Legally, opihi must measure 1¼ inches across to be picked. They cling to rocks with a muscular "foot" that keeps them attached like a suction cup, and are able to withstand even the legendary Hawaiian surf. In part, this is because they carve out mini-depressions in the rocks where they live, although they can move to feed on algae and seaweed. Opihi were harvested by the earliest Hawaiians and remain a popular delicacy, especially at luaus. They are available year-round.

uses, flavor, and cooking qualities

In Hawaii, opihi are usually served raw, and although they are flavorful, they tend to have a chewy texture. Many opihi pickers feast on these delicacies at the shoreline, as the discarded shells there suggest.

substitutions

Periwinkles, abalone, and small clams or oysters.

opihi recipe

North Shore Opihi Poke | 191

roy's fish and seafood

north shore opihi poke

Serves 4 as an appetizer

Diving for opihi around Hawaii's surf-swept, often rocky shoreline is a notoriously dangerous pastime, and every year our local newspapers carry reports of missing or drowned opihi divers. Still, opihi are considered such a delicacy that there are always souls who are brave (or foolish) enough to seek them out. Poke—finely diced, seasoned fresh raw fish or seafood—is a Hawaiian tradition (see the tuna poke recipe on page 127), and many of the fish in this book can be used raw, for sushi, sashimi, or poke. For this recipe, I'd recommend substituting periwinkles or small clams.

    8 ounces shelled opihi
    2 tablespoons minced Maui or other sweet white onion
    2 tablespoons minced ripe tomato
    1 tablespoon minced scallion (green parts only)
    1 tablespoon minced ogo seaweed
    2 tablespoons soy sauce
    1 teaspoon rayu (spicy sesame oil)

Combine all the ingredients in a mixing bowl and toss to mix thoroughly. Refrigerate if not serving immediately.

scallops

(Placopecten magellicanus, Pecten maximus, Chlamys operculris, et al.)

general description

Scallops are filter-feeding bivalve (hinged-shell) mollusks, and there are many varieties of sea scallop in U.S. waters and around the world. The strikingly ridged, fan-shaped scallop shell contains a round adductor muscle (or "eye") that opens and closes the shell, propelling it through the water or along the sea bed. It is this cream-colored to light pink muscle that is eaten; sometimes, orange roe is also attached to the scallop muscle, which is not only edible but delicious. Some types of sea scallop live in shallow water, others on deep open-ocean floors, and they are mostly caught by dredging. Peak season for sea scallops is fall through early spring. Bay scallops, mostly found on the northeast coast of the United States, are much smaller, and most abundant in the fall. Calico scallops are even tinier than bay scallops and more difficult to cook properly.

uses, flavor, and cooking qualities

Typically, there are about 30 shucked sea scallops to the pound, compared with up to 100 of the smaller bay scallops. Because fresh scallops are highly perishable, they are usually shucked immediately at sea, and may not be perfectly fresh when they reach land after several days. "Diver," or "day-boat" scallops, on the other hand, are harvested by hand in shallower water, landed the same day, and are typically the freshest of all. Sea scallops have a pleasantly firm, moist, and meaty texture when not overcooked, and a slightly sweet and delicately complex flavor. Bay scallops are more tender and sweeter in flavor, and consequently, more expensive. While not usually eaten raw (although they can be thinly sliced and served as sashimi), scallops can be "cooked" in citrus juice and served as ceviche. Scallops are relatively low in fat and calories, and they are highly versatile when it comes to cooking methods.

Avoid buying scallops that appear watery, that have an ammonialike odor, or that are bright white in color or clumped together, an indication that they have been soaked in water containing phosphates so they will absorb water and weigh more for market. This means you are buying chemically treated water as well as mushy scallop meat, so try to buy scallops from a reliable source. Some retailers label unsoaked scallops as "dry" scallops, while "fresh frozen" scallops are often preferable to "fresh" scallops of uncertain vintage. If the scallops have a sulphur-like odor, avoid them, as they are beginning to spoil.

substitutions

Clams, oysters, lobster, snapper, and sea bass.

scallop recipes

Spicy Lemongrass-Crusted Scallops on Celery Root Mash with Uni Butter | 195

Asian-Style Bouillabaisse | 196

Seared Day-Boat Scallops with Edamame Mash and Lobster-Truffle Kabayaki | 199

spicy lemongrass-crusted scallops on celery root mash with uni butter

Serves 4 as a main course

Uni—the gland of the spiny sea urchin—has a velvety texture and a sweet, nutty taste. It's a seafood ingredient I love to eat, especially at sushi restaurants. I developed this recipe so I could match the rich flavor of uni with the spicy, lemony crusted scallops. In fact, this recipe has its origins during my time at Le Serene, a restaurant I opened in Burbank during the 1980s, where I paired scallop mousse with sea urchin sauce. For good measure, I have chosen as an accompaniment mashed celery root, a vegetable that I was particularly fond of during my "bell bottom" days. For a source of uni, see page 236.

Uni Butter

2 cups warm beurre blanc (page 223)

3 ounces uni (sea urchin), puréed and strained

¼ cup sake

Salt and freshly ground black pepper

Celery Root Mash

Celery root, peeled and diced (about 2 cups)

Yukon Gold potatoes, peeled and diced (about 2 cups)

2 cups heavy cream

½ cup (1 stick) unsalted butter

Salt and freshly ground black pepper

Scallops

3 tablespoons minced lemongrass (white part only)

1 teaspoon minced garlic

1 teaspoon minced fresh ginger

1 tablespoon shichimi

1½ pounds sea scallops, patted dry

Salt and freshly ground black pepper

3 tablespoons clarified unsalted butter (page 229)

Garnish

1 tablespoon yuzu juice

1 tablespoon soy sauce

1 teaspoon truffle oil

1 cup daikon sprouts or mizuna sprouts

1 package enoki mushrooms (about 3 ounces), trimmed

1 sheet nori, cut into 1 by ½-inch strips

To prepare the uni butter, combine the beurre blanc, uni, sake, and salt and pepper to taste. Keep warm over barely simmering water.

To prepare the mash, cook the celery root and potatoes in separate saucepans of salted boiling water for 15 to 20 minutes, until just tender. Meanwhile, combine the cream and butter in a saucepan and bring to a simmer over low heat. Transfer the celery root and potatoes to a food mill and purée together until smooth (alternatively, whisk by hand). Whisk in the cream mixture and season with salt and pepper to taste. Set aside and keep warm.

continued

continued
from
page 195

To prepare the scallops, combine the lemongrass, garlic, ginger, and shichimi in a bowl. Season the scallops with salt and pepper to taste and crust on one side with the lemongrass mixture. Heat the clarified butter in a heavy sauté pan or skillet set over medium-high heat. Sear the scallops, crusted side down, for 1 minute, until slightly browned. Turn over and sear 1 minute longer, or until golden brown and medium-rare on the inside.

Just before serving, prepare the garnish. Combine all the ingredients in a bowl and toss to combine. Place the mash in the center of warmed plates and arrange the scallops on top of the mash. Spoon the sauce around and garnish with the enoki mixture.

asian-style bouillabaisse

Serves 4 as a main course

When I worked at L'Ermitage, the innovative French restaurant in West Hollywood, many years ago, one of my specialties was a traditional, authentic Provençal bouillabaisse. I couldn't wait for the opportunity to give it a distinctively Asian twist, using ginger, coconut milk, lemongrass, taro, ginger-infused sake, and other ingredients from the Pacific Rim. Bouillabaisse is a dish that lends itself to Hawaiian Fusion cooking, and I recommend adapting the recipe to suit the freshest locally available seafood. For sources of poi, see page 236.

Taro Root Rouille and Croutons

- 1 large egg yolk
- 1 clove roasted garlic (page 228)
- 1 teaspoon freshly squeezed lemon juice
- 6 tablespoons peanut oil, warmed
- ½ cup poi
- Salt and freshly ground black pepper
- 4 diagonally cut slices French baguette bread, ¼ inch thick and about 5 inches long
- 2 tablespoons olive oil
- 1 teaspoon minced garlic

Lobster Stock Base

- 1 tablespoon peanut oil
- 2 cloves garlic, minced
- 1 carrot, peeled and sliced
- 1 stick celery, sliced
- ½ onion, chopped
- ½ stalk lemongrass (white part only), peeled and sliced
- 2 small tomatoes, seeded and diced
- 1 fennel bulb, trimmed, cored, and julienned
- 8 saffron threads
- 3 black peppercorns
- 2 bay leaves
- ½ cup sake
- ¼ cup Pernod
- 4 cups lobster-dashi stock (page 222)

1 tablespoon peanut oil

½ tablespoon minced garlic

½ tablespoon minced fresh ginger

½ Maui or other sweet white onion, julienned

1 leek (white part only), washed and julienned

½ teaspoon minced fresh or frozen kaffir lime leaf

12 day-boat sea scallops

12 shrimp (about 12 ounces total), peeled and deveined

8 ounces mahimahi fillet (or other firm-fleshed white fish), cut into 4 portions

16 mussels, scrubbed and debearded

6 tablespoons sake

½ tablespoon grated mandarin orange zest or regular orange zest

12 baby bok choy leaves

½ tablespoon minced fresh cilantro

Salt and freshly ground black pepper

Preheat the broiler. To prepare the rouille, whisk the egg yolk in a bowl until pale in color. Whisk in the garlic and lemon juice, and while still whisking, gradually drizzle in the warm peanut oil until the mixture thickens and emulsifies. Add the poi and season with salt and pepper to taste. For the croutons, brush the bread slices with the olive oil and sprinkle the garlic on top. Toast under the broiler until golden brown, about 1 minute on each side.

To prepare the lobster stock base, heat the peanut oil in a large, heavy saucepan over medium-high heat. Add the garlic, carrot, celery, onion, lemongrass, tomatoes, fennel, saffron, peppercorns, and bay leaves and sauté for 5 minutes, until soft. Add the sake, Pernod, and stock, and bring to a boil. Decrease the heat to medium-low and simmer for 30 minutes. Strain into a clean bowl and set aside.

Heat the peanut oil in a large, heavy sauté pan or skillet over medium-high heat until hot and shimmering. Add the garlic, ginger, onion, leek, and lime leaf and sauté for 2 minutes, until tender. Add the scallops, shrimp, fish, and mussels and sauté 2 minutes longer, until the scallops and fish are golden brown. Add the sake and stir to deglaze the pan. Add the orange zest, 2½ cups of the reserved lobster stock base, the bok choy, and cilantro. Cook for 2 minutes, until heated. Taste and adjust the seasoning.

Divide the bouillabaisse evenly among warmed bowls. Spread the rouille on the croutons and serve with the bouillabaisse.

seared day-boat scallops with edamame mash and lobster-truffle kabayaki

Serves 4 as an appetizer

This appetizer recipe reminds me of growing up in Japan—my father enjoyed cooking edamame (soybeans) and I would eat them in just about every conceivable way: boiled, spicy, crunchy, you name it. Even when we ate out, I'd seek out edamame. Day-boat scallops, by definition, are the freshest type of scallop available, as they are distributed in fresh form. Typically, other scallops are frozen once caught, and this can compromise flavor and texture. Kabayaki sauce is a popular condiment in Japan, and its sweetness goes perfectly with scallops.

Edamame Mash

4 ounces fresh, cooked and peeled edamame (soybeans)

¼ cup heavy cream

¼ cup unsalted butter

Salt and freshly ground black pepper

Scallops

4 large sea scallops, 6 to 8 ounces total

2 tablespoons olive oil

Shichimi

Salt

Lobster-Truffle Kabayaki

1 cup warm Lobster-Truffle Sauce (page 87)

2 tablespoons kabayaki sauce

To prepare the mash, cook the edamame in a saucepan of salted boiling water for about 10 minutes, or until soft. Drain, reserve 4 beans for garnish, and purée the rest with a potato masher or a whisk. Transfer to a clean saucepan and add the cream and butter. Season with salt and pepper to taste. Set aside and keep warm.

To prepare the scallops, coat them with the oil, then sprinkle with shichimi and salt to taste. Heat a dry large nonstick sauté pan for 2 minutes over high heat. Add the scallops and cook for about 1 1/2 minutes on each side, or until golden brown and medium-rare on the inside. Transfer to warmed plates. Pour the lobster-truffle sauce around the scallops, drizzle with the kabayaki, and serve with the edamame mash. Garnish each serving with a whole, reserved soybean.

shrimp

(Penaeus and many other genuses)

general description

Shrimp (also marketed as "prawns" in Europe and in some regions of the United States) is a ten-legged crustacean and the most abundant type of harvested shellfish worldwide. In the United States, shrimp is the most important kind of seafood commercially after canned tuna, with Texas and Louisiana accounting for the largest landings in terms of value. Even so, a majority of the shrimp consumed in the United States is imported. There are many types of North American shrimp, and the four most popular are pink shrimp (*Penaeus duorarum*), white shrimp (*Penaeus setiferus*), brown shrimp (*Penaeus aztecus*), and blue shrimp (*Penaeus stylirostris*), all of which are harvested along the Eastern seaboard and the Gulf Coast. Notable among imported shrimp are Asian varieties such as tiger shrimp (*Penaeus monodon*) and Chinese white shrimp (*Penaeus chinensis*). These are all warm-water shrimp that typically live in shallow water. Our local Hawaiian blue prawn (*Macrobranchium rosenbergii*) is a farmed freshwater shrimp native to Malaysia.

A significant amount of the shrimp consumed in the United States is imported and farm-raised; however, most of the North American catch, which peaks in the summer months, is wild. Without question, my preference is for fresh local shrimp, which has a superior flavor and firm texture, but otherwise, I find there is not a great deal of difference in appearance or quality between species or sources. In any case, most shrimp is frozen before it reaches consumers.

uses, flavor, and cooking qualities

Other than fresh local shrimp, I recommend buying frozen shrimp (whole shrimp with heads on, in the shell) rather than frozen-and-thawed or peeled shrimp. The exception to this rule is the smaller cold-water rock shrimp (*Sicyonia brevirostris*), which is usually sold peeled and headless due to the difficulty in removing its shell. Defrost shrimp gradually, in the refrigerator or in a bowl of cold water; never thaw at room temperature. Defrosting in the microwave will compromise texture. Once defrosted, wash the shrimp in saltwater to help give it a cleaner flavor.

Shrimp is typically sold by size: small, medium, large, extra-large, jumbo, and colossal; or by the number sold per pound, such as "31 to 40s" (medium), "21 to 30s" (large), "16 to 20s" (extra large), "12 to 15s" (jumbo), or "U-12s" (under 12 to a pound, usually marketed as colossal shrimp). Note that for every pound of whole shrimp in the shell, the yield of cooked, shelled shrimp meat will be just over 8 ounces.

Avoid shrimp with an ammonialike odor or black spots on the shells, both of which are signs of deterioration. Once thawed, shrimp appears translucent; when cooked, it turns opaque and whitish-pink in color. Its flavor ranges from delicate and mild to nutty, and the texture when cooked should be firm yet tender; beware of overcooking shrimp, as it will dry out and become rubbery. Shrimp is highly versatile, and can be grilled (preferably, with shells on), sautéed, fried, boiled, poached, and baked.

substitutions

Other shellfish, such as lobster, scallops, and crab; and firmly textured white-fleshed fish, such as swordfish, ono, and snapper.

shrimp recipes

shrimp salad with avocado and green papaya

Serves 4 as an appetizer

Green papaya salad is virtually a trademark dish in Thai cuisine, and this is my "new wave" version. Once again, I have used contrasting flavors and textures: the soft richness of avocado, crunchy lush papaya and nuts, warm, fragrant shrimp, and cool salad ingredients.

3 tablespoons salt

2 small green papayas (about 10 ounces total), peeled, seeded, and julienned

1 tablespoon dried shrimp

2 red Thai chiles, seeded and minced

1/4 teaspoon minced garlic

3 tablespoons diced macadamia nuts, toasted (page 228)

3 tablespoons freshly squeezed lime juice

1 tablespoon sugar plus 1 teaspoon

2 tablespoons fish sauce

2 tablespoons sesame oil

1 tablespoon canola oil

16 extra-large shrimp (about 1 pound), peeled and deveined

1 teaspoon minced garlic

1/2 teaspoon minced fresh ginger

1 tablespoon minced scallion (white part only)

16 fresh mint leaves

4 large radicchio leaves

1 avocado, halved, pitted, peeled, and cut into 4 fans

Stir the salt into a bowl of cold water and add the julienned papaya. Soak for about 1 hour. Meanwhile, put the dried shrimp in a small bowl and cover with hot water. Let soak for 1 hour; drain, mince, and set aside. Drain the papaya, rinse under cold running water, drain again, and pat dry. Transfer the papaya to a bowl and add the minced dried shrimp. Add the chiles, garlic, 2 tablespoons of the macadamia nuts, the lime juice, the 1 tablespoon sugar, and 1 tablespoon of the fish sauce. Toss to thoroughly combine.

Heat the sesame oil and canola oil in a heavy sauté pan or skillet over medium-high heat. Add the shrimp, garlic, ginger, and scallion and sauté for 2 minutes. Add the remaining 1 tablespoon fish sauce and stir to deglaze the pan. Add the 1 teaspoon sugar and the mint and sauté 30 seconds longer.

To serve, arrange the radicchio leaves on plates. Place the papaya mixture in the radicchio "cups" and arrange an avocado fan on top of each serving. Place 4 shrimp on top of each salad. Garnish the salads with the remaining 1 tablespoon macadamia nuts.

minced shrimp and macadamia nut appetizer with crisp pineapple

Serves 4 as an appetizer

This is my Pacific Rim version of salsa and chips! For this recipe, I was inspired by watching our corporate pastry chef at Roy's, Noah French, making some crisp pineapple rings in the kitchen for a dessert garnish. I thought the rings would make an ideal base for a canapé-style appetizer, and this is the result.

Crisp Pineapple

- 2 cups sugar
- 2 cups water
- 1 small pineapple, peeled, cored, and very finely sliced (about ⅛ inch)

Shrimp

- 2 teaspoons olive oil
- 1 pound shrimp, peeled, deveined, and diced
- 1 tomato, peeled, seeded, and finely diced (page 228)
- 1 small avocado, halved, pitted, peeled, and diced

Shrimp, continued

- 2 tablespoons minced Maui or other sweet white onion
- 1 tablespoon thawed frozen passion fruit concentrate
- 1 teaspoon finely sliced scallion (green parts only)
- 1 teaspoon minced fresh cilantro
- 1 teaspoon Tabasco sauce, or to taste
- Salt and freshly ground black pepper
- ¼ cup macadamia nuts, toasted (page 228)

Preheat the oven to 250°F. To prepare the pineapple, combine the sugar and water in a saucepan and stir to dissolve the sugar. Bring to a boil over high heat, decrease the heat to low, and simmer for 5 minutes. Add the pineapple slices and simmer for about 10 minutes, or until translucent. Carefully remove with a slotted spoon and drain on paper towels. Transfer the pineapple slices to a baking sheet lined with parchment paper and bake for about 20 minutes, or until dry on top and golden brown on the edge. Turn the slices over and bake 20 minutes longer, or until golden brown and crispy. Remove from the oven and let cool. When cool, cut the slices into triangles and set aside.

To prepare the shrimp, heat the oil in a heavy nonstick sauté pan or skillet over medium-high heat. Add the shrimp and stir-fry for 45 seconds to 1 minute, or until evenly pink. Transfer to a bowl and add the tomato, avocado, onion, passion fruit concentrate, scallion, cilantro, Tabasco, and salt and pepper to taste. Mix well, spoon onto warmed bowls, and sprinkle with the macadamia nuts. Serve with the pineapple triangles.

stir-fried spicy kauai prawns with mint

Serves 4 as an appetizer, 2 as a main course

A few years ago, there was a thriving aquaculture business on Oahu's North Shore that raised plenty of succulent shrimp. I liked the product, especially because it was a local enterprise and fresh shrimp is definitely preferable to frozen. After that local business closed down, we found another great source, from Kekaha on the Waimea side of Kauai. I filmed a segment for my PBS TV program at the shrimp farm there, and I used this particular recipe for our anniversary dinner at Roy's in Tokyo. The cooling quality of the mint contrasts very well with the sweet shrimp and heat of the chiles.

Prawns

2 tablespoons fish sauce

1 tablespoon soy sauce

2 tablespoons freshly squeezed lime juice

2 tablespoons sugar

12 extra-large shrimp (about 12 ounces total), peeled and deveined

2 tablespoons olive oil

3 tablespoons sesame oil

½ yellow onion, finely sliced

1 red bell pepper, seeded, deribbed, and julienned

1 green bell pepper, seeded, deribbed, and julienned

8 scallions, sliced (green and white parts)

2 tablespoons minced fresh ginger

Prawns, continued

2 tablespoons minced garlic

1 small red Thai chile, seeded and minced (or more to taste)

24 fresh mint leaves

24 fresh cilantro leaves

1 cup mung bean sprouts

1 to 2 tablespoons water

Egg Noodles

1 tablespoon peanut oil

1 tablespoon dark sesame oil

12 ounces fresh thin Chinese egg noodles

2 tablespoons water

4 mint sprigs, for garnish

In a small bowl, combine the fish sauce, soy sauce, lime juice, and sugar, stirring until the sugar dissolves. Add the shrimp, cover with the mixture, and refrigerate for 30 minutes. Heat the olive oil in a wok or large, heavy skillet over high heat until almost smoking. Add the shrimp (reserve the marinade) and sear for about 1 minute on each side, or until pink. Remove the shrimp with tongs and drain on paper towels. Wipe out the wok with paper towels and add the sesame oil. Heat until just smoking. Add the onion, red and green bell peppers, scallions, ginger, garlic, and chile. Stir-fry for 1 minute, and then return the prawns to the wok and add the mint. Pour in the reserved marinade and stir to deglaze the wok. Add the cilantro and bean sprouts, and up to 2 tablespoons of water if the sauce tastes too salty or lemony. Set aside and keep warm.

To prepare the egg noodles, heat the peanut oil and sesame oil in a heavy sauté pan or skillet over medium-high heat until hot and shimmering. Add the egg noodles and cook for about 2 minutes, or until heated through. Carefully add the water and let the noodles "steam" until the water evaporates. Transfer the noodles to warmed plates and spoon the shrimp mixture on top. Garnish with the mint sprigs.

macaroni and cheese with shrimp and truffles

Serves 4 as a main course

This is a disarmingly simple recipe that combines comfort food with a sense of luxury, by means of the truffle butter and shrimp. At Roy's, we serve a lot of macaroni and cheese for the *keikis*—our younger guests—and I figured we should serve a grown-up version for adult "mac & cheese" lovers. The idea for it originated with older *keikis* who requested shrimp with the mac & cheese, and I just took it a step further. The truffle butter makes twice as much as is needed; use leftover butter for pasta dishes, ravioli, or for finishing shellfish. You don't have to mold it, especially if you are using it immediately, but it makes a nice presentation and it is easier to store that way.

Truffle Butter

¼ cup Madeira wine

2 tablespoons minced black truffle

½ cup (1 stick) butter, softened

1 teaspoon salt

½ teaspoon freshly cracked black pepper

Macaroni and Cheese with Shrimp

1 pound macaroni

¼ cup minced shallots

4 teaspoons minced garlic

½ cup dry white wine

2½ cups half-and-half

3 cups (12 ounces) shredded Cheddar cheese

20 shrimp (about 1¼ pounds total), peeled and deveined

To prepare the truffle butter, combine the Madeira and truffle in a small saucepan. Bring to a boil, decrease the heat to medium, and cook to reduce the liquid by half. Transfer to a bowl, add the butter, salt, and pepper, and whisk until thoroughly blended. Place the mixture on a square of parchment paper or aluminum foil. Fold the paper to mold the mixture into a cylinder about 1/2-inch in diameter. Use now, or refrigerate for up to two weeks in an airtight container.

continued

continued
from
page 207

In a large pot of salted boiling water, cook the macaroni until al dente, about 5 minutes. Drain. Set aside and keep warm.

Meanwhile, melt half of the truffle butter in a saucepan over medium heat. Add the shallots and garlic and sauté for about 2 minutes, or until softened. Add the white wine and stir to deglaze the pan. Add the half-and-half and bring to a boil. Add the cheese and stir until it melts and the mixture is smooth. Add the shrimp and cooked macaroni and cook for about 2 minutes longer, or until the shrimp is evenly pink. Transfer to warmed plates.

shrimp and chicken dumplings with mango and mint dipping sauce

Serves 4 as an appetizer

One of my favorite Chinese foods is shiu mai—little dumplings often served as dim sum—and this recipe is derived from that tradition. You can make the dumplings with just shrimp or chicken, but I prefer the mixture of flavors, and the combination keeps the cost down. The dipping sauce is a great way to use the lush, ripe mangoes that come into season in Hawaii in early summer, and the sauce is extremely versatile—I like to use it for satays, spring rolls, and grilled chicken or fried chicken wings. Note that the dried mushrooms in this recipe should be soaked and rehydrated overnight.

Dipping Sauce

½ cup mango purée

2 garlic cloves, minced to a paste

1 fresh red Thai chile, seeded and minced

2 tablespoons sugar

2 tablespoons freshly squeezed lemon juice

2 tablespoons fish sauce

1 tablespoon finely diced macadamia nuts, toasted (page 228)

1 tablespoon julienned fresh mint

Soy sauce to taste (optional)

Water as needed (optional)

Dumplings

12 ounces ground chicken

12 ounces shrimp, peeled, deveined, and diced

1 teaspoon dried chicken bouillon powder or stock base

1 teaspoon sugar

½ teaspoon freshly ground white pepper

4 garlic cloves, minced

1 tablespoon finely grated fresh ginger

8 dried shiitake mushrooms, soaked in water overnight and minced

2 tablespoons fish sauce

1 teaspoon salt

Water as needed (optional)

½ tablespoon cornstarch

1 tablespoon water

20 square wonton wrappers

To prepare the dipping sauce, combine all the ingredients except the water in a bowl. Stir until thoroughly combined. Let stand for at least 30 minutes to allow the flavors to develop. Add a little water, if desired, to thin the sauce.

To prepare the dumplings, put the chicken in the bowl of an electric mixer fitted with the paddle attachment. Mix the chicken for 5 minutes and then add the shrimp. Add the bouillon powder, sugar, pepper, garlic, ginger, shiitakes, and fish sauce and mix 1 minute longer. Season with the salt and if necessary, add a little cold water to soften the mixture.

Bring 1 inch of water to a boil in the bottom of a steamer. Mix the cornstarch and water in a cup. Meanwhile, lay out the wonton wrappers on a work surface. Place 2 tablespoons of the dumpling mixture in the center of each. Brush a little of the cornstarch mixture around the edge of each wrapper and carefully transfer the wrapper to the palm of your hand. Curl your fingers around the wrapper so the filling forms a pocket, and with your other hand, gather and twist the top of the wrapper to secure tightly. Repeat for the remaining dumplings. Transfer to the steamer, cover, and steam the dumplings for 6 to 8 minutes, until cooked through.

Transfer the dipping sauce to individual ramekins. Arrange 5 dumplings on each serving plate and serve with the dipping sauce.

spicy tempura shrimp with mango-avocado salad

Serves 4 as an appetizer

The tropical flavors of mango and avocado are about as different as you can get, but both have a richness and lushness, and they make a great combination. Shrimp goes well with both, so this is a natural pairing. The tempura (batter) crust gives the shrimp an appealing crispness to contrast with the smooth texture of the salad, and it provides a definite Asian flair to the whole dish.

Chile Sauce

½ cup mayonnaise

2 tablespoons sriracha

2 teaspoons fish sauce

Spicy Tempura Shrimp

1 large egg yolk

1 cup ice water

½ cup all-purpose flour

3½ cups canola oil

½ cup dark sesame oil

1 pound extra-large shrimp (about 16), peeled and deveined

½ cup cornstarch

Salt

Mango-Avocado Salad

4 large radicchio leaf "cups"

1 large ripe mango, peeled, pitted, and julienned

1 ripe avocado, halved, pitted, peeled, and diced

1 tablespoon tobiko caviar, for garnish

4 scallions (green and white parts), finely slivered, for garnish

To prepare the chile sauce, combine all the ingredients in a bowl. Stir to blend. Cover and refrigerate.

To prepare the shrimp, whisk together the egg yolk and ice water in a bowl. Stir in the flour and mix until a batter forms. Heat the canola oil and sesame oil in a deep fryer or large, heavy saucepan and heat to 375°F. With a sharp knife, score the underside of the shrimp and straighten out the tail. Put the cornstarch on a plate and season with salt to taste. Using tongs, dip the shrimp in the cornstarch and then in the tempura batter, and carefully place in the hot pan. Deep-fry the shrimp for about 2 minutes, in batches or until golden brown. Remove with tongs and drain on paper towels.

To serve, arrange the julienned mango on the plate and place the radicchio leaves on top. Place the avocado and cooked shrimp in the leaves and drizzle some of the sauce over the shrimp. Sprinkle the tobiko over the sauce. Serve with the remaining sauce on the side and garnish with the scallions.

squid

calamari

(Loligo opalescens et al.)

general description

Although there are many varieties of squid, the main ones marketed in the United States are the Pacific squid (*Loligo opalescens*) and the Atlantic squid (*Loligo pealei*). Squid are cephalopods in the mollusk family, a group that also includes the octopus. They have eight "arms" and two longer tentacles with which they feed, and are semitransparent in the water. They can change color to hide from prey, and can squirt a dark ink to further confuse attackers. They tend to congregate in large groups, or schools, and they are typically caught with seine nets or trawls.

flavor, uses, and cooking qualities

Squid, also referred to by its Italian name, calamari, is considered a delicacy in Mediterranean countries and in Japan, and it has become an increasingly popular type of seafood in U.S. restaurants. Most "fresh" squid has in fact been frozen and thawed, a process that does not affect the flavor or texture if done properly. Whole squid should smell fresh and briny; they should appear shiny, be white or gray in color, and should be firmly textured. I recommend buying already cleaned squid, as cleaning your own is time-consuming. Squid is also sold already cut into rings.

Cooked squid has a chewy texture and a mildly sweet, somewhat nutlike flavor; like other mollusks, overcooking will result in a rubbery texture (as will undercooking). I prefer smaller, rather than larger squid, as they are usually softer in texture. I recommend spending a little more and using Japanese sushi-grade calamari, which is even more tender. Try and research a good source (or use one listed on page 236), or buy your calamari from a sushi restaurant. Fresh squid is available most of the year, but tends to be less abundant during fall months.

substitutions

Clams and scallops.

squid recipes

rigatoni of calamari with garlic-shiso sauce

Serves 4 as an appetizer

This appetizer recipe is inspired by my friend and master chef Nobu Matsuhisa, who prepares calamari so that it resembles rigatoni. Cutting open calamari tubes and scoring them in a crisscross pattern makes them curl up nicely when cooked. Shiso is an herb native to China that is popular in Japanese cooking and used increasingly in Hawaiian Fusion cuisine (see page 234). The flavors of shiso and garlic go together wonderfully well, and although shiso has no direct substitute, you can use basil instead with impressive results. You can use the sauce with most fish. Black fungus can be found in the Chinese food section of supermarkets, or in Asian stores; it is also marketed as cloud ear mushrooms. Its texture adds an extra element to the sauce.

Calamari

- 1 pound cleaned calamari tubes (about 20)
- 3 tablespoons olive oil

Garlic-Shiso Sauce

- 2 tablespoons olive oil
- 2 teaspoons minced garlic
- 1 cup diagonally cut asparagus tips
- 1 cup sliced shiitake mushrooms caps
- 2 tablespoons julienned black fungus, rehydrated in warm water and drained

Garlic-Shiso Sauce, continued

- ¼ cup soy sauce
- 6 tablespoons sake
- 2 tablespoons yuzu juice, or 1 tablespoon lemon juice and 1 tablespoon orange juice
- ⅓ cup unsalted butter, softened
- 4 fresh shiso leaves, or 6 large fresh basil leaves, julienned
- ½ teaspoon salt
- ½ teaspoon freshly ground white pepper
- ½ tablespoon shichimi

To prepare the calamari, cut open one side of each calamari tube with a sharp knife. Lay flat and pat dry. Cut the tube in half lengthwise and then score each piece in a crisscross pattern with about 1/16 inch between each score mark. Heat the 3 tablespoons olive oil in a large sauté pan or skillet over medium-high heat until almost smoking. Add the calamari and sauté for about 2 minutes, or until they start to roll up. Remove the calamari, drain on paper towels, and set aside.

To prepare the sauce, heat the 2 tablespoons olive oil in a large nonstick sauté pan or skillet over medium-high heat. Add the garlic and sauté for 2 to 3 minutes, until it begins to turn golden brown. Add the asparagus, shiitakes, and black fungus and sauté for 2 to 3 minutes longer, until the mushrooms are almost tender. Add the cooked calamari and stir in the soy sauce, sake, and yuzu. Add the butter and stir until it is melted and incorporated. Add the shiso, salt, pepper, and shichimi and stir well. Divide the mixture evenly among warmed bowls.

roy's crisp lemongrass calamari salad

Serves 4 to 6 as a main course

This is a simplified version of a popular salad that we feature on our menu at Roy's. You can make the salad with clams or oysters, if you prefer, and the noodles and dressing make a great bed for fish or chicken served as a main course, or prepared as a side dish. Likewise, any leftover dressing can be used on salads or as a sauce for fish. The translucent bean thread noodles are made with dried mung beans.

Lemongrass Dressing

- 2 tablespoons olive oil
- 1 teaspoon minced garlic
- ½ small yellow onion, finely grated
- 2 tablespoons finely grated daikon
- 2 tablespoons minced fresh cilantro
- 1½ tablespoons minced lemongrass (white part only)
- 1½ tablespoons finely grated fresh ginger
- 3 fresh or frozen kaffir lime leaves
- ½ cup freshly squeezed orange juice
- ¼ cup freshly squeezed lemon juice
- 2 tablespoons freshly squeezed lime juice
- 6 tablespoons rice wine vinegar
- ¼ cup soy sauce
- 1½ tablespoons fish sauce
- 1 tablespoon sriracha
- Salt and freshly ground black pepper

Noodles

- 6 ounces dried bean thread noodles
- 1 tablespoon dark sesame oil
- 3 tablespoons oyster sauce
- 2 tablespoons fish sauce
- ½ cup minced scallions (including green parts)
- ½ green bell pepper, seeded, deribbed, and julienned
- ½ red bell pepper, seeded, deribbed, and julienned
- ½ yellow bell pepper, seeded, deribbed, and julienned
- 1 small carrot, peeled and finely julienned
- 2 teaspoons finely minced lemongrass (white part only)
- 1 teaspoon shichimi

Calamari

- 2 pounds calamari, cleaned
- 6 large eggs
- 2 cups all-purpose flour
- 2 cups panko (Japanese bread crumbs)
- 1½ cups (6 ounces) finely grated Parmesan cheese
- 4 cups canola oil
- 1 head butter leaf lettuce

To prepare the dressing for the noodles, heat the olive oil in a heavy saucepan over medium-high heat. Add the garlic and sauté for 30 seconds, until fragrant. Remove from the heat and add the onion, daikon, cilantro, lemongrass, ginger, and lime leaves. Stir in the orange juice, lemon juice, lime juice, vinegar, soy sauce, fish sauce, and sriracha. Return to medium heat and bring to a boil. Decrease the heat and simmer for 2 minutes, or until the lemongrass and lime leaves are soft. Transfer to a blender, purée, and strain into a bowl. Season with salt and pepper to taste and set aside.

To prepare the noodles, soak the noodles in a bowl of warm water for 10 minutes. Bring a saucepan of water to a boil, add the noodles, and cook for 4 to 5 minutes, until the noodles turn transparent. Drain the noodles and rinse under cold running water to stop the cooking process. Transfer to a bowl and add ½ cup of the lemongrass dressing. Add the sesame oil, oyster sauce, fish sauce, scallions, red, green, and yellow bell pepper, carrot, lemongrass, and shichimi and mix well. Set aside.

To prepare the calamari, cut the calamari tubes into 2-inch rings and reserve the tentacles. Beat the eggs in a bowl and place the flour on a plate. On a separate plate, mix together the panko and cheese. Dredge the calamari in the flour, and then dip in the beaten egg. Next, dredge the calamari in the panko mixture and set aside on a clean plate. Refrigerate for 10 minutes. Heat the canola oil to 375°F in a deep fryer or large, heavy saucepan. Fry the calamari in small batches until golden brown, about 1½ minutes per batch.

Arrange the lettuce as a bed on serving plates and top with the noodles. Add the crisp calamari and serve the remaining dressing on the side.

basic recipes
and techniques

chicken stock

Makes about 4 cups

You can use this basic poultry stock recipe for duck or turkey bones. For duck stock, substitute 1 or 2 duck carcasses for the chicken; for turkey stock, use 1 carcass and double the remaining ingredients for double the yield.

1 or 2 chicken carcasses, broken up
2 tablespoons olive oil
1 stalk celery, coarsely chopped
½ cup coarsely chopped yellow onion
½ cup peeled and coarsely chopped carrot
1 gallon water
¼ cup fresh basil leaves
¼ cup fresh thyme leaves
5 black peppercorns
2 bay leaves
Salt and freshly ground black pepper

Preheat the oven to 350°F. Place the chicken bones in a roasting pan and sprinkle with 1½ tablespoons of the oil. Roast in the oven until brown, 15 to 20 minutes. Heat the remaining ½ tablespoon oil in a stockpot over medium-high heat. Add the celery, onion, and carrot and sauté for 5 minutes, until softened. Add the water, basil, thyme, peppercorns, bay leaves, and roasted chicken bones and bring to a boil. Decrease the heat and simmer until the liquid is reduced to about 4 cups, about 45 minutes. Periodically skim the surface of the stock to remove any impurities. Strain, discard the solids, and season with salt and pepper to taste. Store in an airtight container in the refrigerator for up to 3 days, or freeze for up to 3 months.

veal stock

Makes about 8 cups

For an even more intense flavor, use more bones, but be sure to keep them covered with water while cooking.

1 to 2 pounds veal bones
¼ cup coarsely chopped celery
¼ cup peeled and coarsely chopped carrot
½ cup coarsely chopped yellow onion
½ cup coarsely chopped tomatoes
2 tablespoons coarsely chopped mushroom stems or caps
2 cloves garlic
1 tablespoon tomato purée
½ cup fresh basil leaves
½ teaspoon minced fresh thyme
1 bay leaf, crumbled
3 black peppercorns
1 gallon water
Salt and freshly ground black pepper

Preheat the oven to 350°F. Put the veal bones in a roasting pan and add the celery, carrot, onion, tomatoes, mushroom stems, garlic, tomato purée, basil, thyme, bay leaf, and peppercorns. Stir the vegetable mixture together. Roast in the oven until dark brown, 20 to 30 minutes. Transfer to a stockpot, add the water, and bring to a boil. Decrease the heat and simmer until reduced to about 8 cups, about 25 to 30 minutes. Periodically skim the surface of the stock to remove any impurities. Strain, discard the solids, and season with salt and pepper to taste. Store in an airtight container in the refrigerator for up to 3 days, or freeze for up to 3 months.

demi-glace

Makes about 2 cups

If you are short of time, by all means buy a good-quality commercial demi-glace, but making your own from scratch is a very satisfying experience. There are two routes you can take; one is to start with the veal stock recipe on page 220 and cook to reduce it over low heat until thick enough to coat the back of a spoon. However, if you are using veal shanks, which have a relatively high protein and gelatin content, the stock will thicken before a full flavor has time to emerge. For these reasons, my preference is to start with beef short ribs, which are low in gelatin and high in flavor.

2 tablespoons canola oil

1 large yellow onion, chopped

2 stalks celery, sliced

1 large carrot, peeled and sliced

5 pounds beef short ribs

½ cup tomato paste

3 bay leaves

2½ gallons water

Salt and freshly ground black pepper

Heat the canola oil in a heavy sauté pan or skillet over medium-high heat. Add the onion, celery, and carrot and sauté for about 5 minutes, or until the onion turns golden brown. Transfer to a large stockpot and add the ribs, the tomato paste, bay leaves, and water. Bring to a boil, decrease the heat to low, and simmer for 3 to 4 hours, periodically skimming the surface of the stock to remove any impurities. Strain, discard the solids, and transfer to a clean saucepan. Season with salt and pepper to taste and cook over low heat to reduce to about 2 cups; the demi-glace should be thick enough to coat the back of a spoon. You can freeze it for up to 3 months.

lobster-dashi stock

This Japanese-influenced stock provides a foundation for a number of wonderfully flavorful sauces to match most kinds of shellfish or fish. Dashi, kombu, bonito, dried mushrooms, and dried shrimp can be purchased at Asian markets.

1 tablespoon canola oil

1 large yellow onion, coarsely chopped

2 stalks celery, coarsely chopped

½ carrot, peeled and roughly chopped

2½ pounds lobster shells and heads, split

1 gallon water

1 piece kombu seaweed (3 inches square)

3 dried shiitake mushrooms

2 tablespoons dried shrimp

1 tablespoon soy sauce

2 tablespoons dashi, or to taste

1 teaspoon bonito flakes

Heat the oil in a large, heavy saucepan over medium-high heat until hot and shimmering. Add the onion, celery, and carrot and cook for 2 to 3 minutes, until soft. Add the lobster shells and heads and sauté for about 5 minutes, stirring occasionally. Add the water, kombu, shiitakes, dried shrimp, soy, and dashi and cook for 15 to 20 minutes longer, or until about 4 cups liquid remain; add the bonito flakes and cook 10 minutes longer. Strain through cheesecloth, repeating if necessary, until the stock is clear.

beurre blanc

Makes about 3/4 cup

This classic and wonderfully adaptable sauce is the foundation for many other sauces in my Hawaiian Fusion repertoire.

½ cup dry white wine
2 teaspoons white wine vinegar
1 teaspoon freshly squeezed lemon juice
1 tablespoon minced shallot
2 tablespoons heavy cream
½ cup (1 stick) cold unsalted butter, chopped
¼ teaspoon salt
Freshly ground white pepper

Combine the wine, vinegar, lemon juice, and shallot in a heavy stainless-steel saucepan. Bring to a boil over medium-high heat and cook to reduce the liquid until it becomes syrupy. Add the cream and cook to reduce by half. Decrease the heat to low and gradually add the butter, stirring slowly; do not whisk. Take care not to let the mixture boil, or it will separate. When the butter is incorporated, season with salt and pepper to taste, and strain through a fine-mesh sieve into the top of a double boiler. Keep warm over barely simmering water.

homemade teriyaki sauce

Makes about 1½ cups

You can buy teriyaki sauce, but it's easy enough to make at home.

1 cup soy sauce
1 tablespoon minced garlic
1 tablespoon minced fresh ginger
1 cup sugar

Combine all the ingredients in a heavy saucepan and bring to a simmer over medium-high heat. Decrease the heat to low and simmer for about 15 minutes, stirring occasionally, until the liquid is syrupy and reduced to about 1½ cups. Store in an airtight container in the refrigerator for up to 1 month.

lobster paste

Makes about ¹/₂ cup

This recipe makes a great "base" flavoring for many other sauces and dishes.

1 tablespoon peanut oil

½ yellow onion, chopped

½ carrot, peeled and chopped

½ stalk celery, chopped

8 ounces lobster shells, or 2 Maine lobster heads

2 cloves garlic, minced

1 small tomato, chopped

2 or 3 sprigs flat-leaf parsley

½ teaspoon chopped fresh tarragon

½ cup dry white wine

6 cups water

Heat the peanut oil in a large, heavy saucepan over medium heat. Add the onion, carrot, and celery, and sauté for about 2 minutes, or until semi-soft. Stir in the lobster shells, garlic, tomato, parsley, and tarragon. Add the wine and stir to deglaze the pan. Bring to a simmer and cook for 5 minutes. Add the water and bring to a boil over high heat. Decrease the heat to medium-low and simmer 30 minutes longer. Strain into a clean saucepan, discarding the vegetables. Transfer the shells to a blender and add enough of the strained broth to make blending possible. Blend until pulverized, and then strain the liquid back into the pan through a fine-mesh sieve. Bring to a simmer over medium heat and cook to reduce to about ½ cup. Store in the refrigerator for up to 2 weeks or in the freezer for up to 6 months.

scallion oil

Makes about 1 cup

5 scallions, cut into fine slivers (green parts only)
1 cup olive oil
Salt and freshly ground black pepper

Prepare an ice bath in a large bowl. Cook the scallion slivers in a small saucepan of boiling water for about 30 seconds, or until slightly wilted. Drain the scallions and transfer to the ice bath to stop the cooking process. Drain again and transfer to a blender. Add the oil and salt and pepper to taste and purée until smooth. Strain through a fine-mesh sieve into a bowl, and then transfer to an airtight bottle or container. Store in the refrigerator for up to 1 week.

lomi lomi tomatoes

Makes about 1 1/2 cups

In the Hawaiian language, the word lomi means "crush" or "massage," and in this recipe, it refers to the finely diced tomatoes. The similarly prepared traditional dish of lomi lomi salmon is a popular luau item here in Hawaii. This is a versatile salsa that is best used fresh.

6 ounces tomatoes, peeled, seeded, and finely diced (see page 228)
1/4 cup minced Maui or other sweet white onion
2 tablespoons minced fresh chives
1 tablespoon rayu (spicy sesame oil)
1 teaspoon white or red Hawaiian salt
1/4 teaspoon freshly ground black pepper

Combine all the ingredients in a bowl and stir gently to blend. Cover and refrigerate for at least 1 hour. Use within 1 or 2 days.

hawaiian chile water

Makes about 1¹/₂ cups

This is a popular condiment that you'll find on diner and restaurant tables across the state. It uses fresh small Hawaiian red chiles, but other chiles can be substituted.

2 cups water

8 small Hawaiian or Fiesta chiles, 1 red jalapeño, or 2 red Serrano chiles, halved and seeded

1 teaspoon grated fresh ginger

1 teaspoon minced garlic

1 teaspoon salt

Combine all the ingredients in a saucepan. Bring to a boil, decrease the heat to low, and simmer for 10 minutes. Remove from the heat and let cool. Transfer the mixture to a blender and purée for 40 seconds. Store in an airtight bottle or container in the refrigerator for up to 1 month.

mashed potatoes

Serves 4 to 6 as a side dish

Here's a classic comfort food recipe that goes with most of the dishes in this book. These potatoes have just a touch of garlic; increase the amount of garlic for those who enjoy the flavor, or leave it out completely, if you prefer.

2 pounds potatoes, peeled and chopped

½ tablespoon salt

1 teaspoon unsalted butter, plus 2 tablespoons

½ teaspoon minced garlic, or to taste

1 cup milk

Salt and freshly ground black pepper

Preheat the oven to 300°F. Bring a saucepan of cold water to a boil over medium heat, add the potatoes and salt, and cook for 15 to 20 minutes, until tender. Drain the potatoes and put them in an ovenproof bowl. Beat with an electric mixer until smooth and fluffy. Place in the oven for 2 to 3 minutes so the excess moisture evaporates.

Melt the 1 teaspoon butter in a small saucepan over low heat and sauté the garlic for 30 seconds. Stir the garlic and butter into the potatoes. Add the 2 tablespoons butter and the milk to the same saucepan and bring to a boil over medium-high heat. Stir the mixture into the potatoes and then whisk until thoroughly combined and smooth, about 2 minutes if using an electric mixer at medium speed, or longer if whisking by hand. Season with salt and pepper to taste.

steamed rice

Makes about 6 cups; serves 4 to 6 as a side dish

At Roy's, we usually offer a side of steamed white Japanese rice with our fish and seafood main courses. Japanese rice is a short-grain rice with a starchier, stickier texture than that of long-grain rice. It is available in most supermarkets under various brand names, such as Calrose (it may also be labeled "medium-grain"). My preference is to use an automatic rice cooker because it makes the process so simple, eliminating any guesswork. It's well worth the investment— just follow the instructions and you are all set. Of course, you can also use a saucepan and cook the rice on the stove top.

2 cups Japanese short-grain rice
2 cups water

Put the rice in a fine-mesh sieve and rinse under cold running water several times, until the water runs clear. Drain the rice and transfer to a bowl. Cover with fresh cold water and let soak for 1 hour. Drain the rice; if using a rice cooker, place the rice in the cooker, add water to the 2-cup mark, cover, and turn the cooker on.

Alternatively, to cook the rice on the stove top, place the rice in a saucepan and add the water. Bring to a boil, decrease the heat, cover, and cook until the rice is soft and sticky and the water has just evaporated, about 15 minutes.

roasted garlic

Roasting garlic diminishes its pungency and bitterness, and brings out a sweeter, more mellow flavor.

    1 garlic bulb, top ¼ inch sliced off horizontally
    1 tablespoon olive oil
    Salt and freshly ground black pepper

Preheat the oven to 350°F. Place the head of garlic in a roasting pan, drizzle with the oil, and sprinkle with salt and pepper to taste. Roast in the oven for 25 to 30 minutes, until soft. Remove and let cool.

toasting seeds and nuts

Roasting brings out the full flavors and aromas of seeds and nuts, giving them a pleasing complexity. The techniques involved are pretty simple.

For macadamia nuts: Preheat the oven to 300°F. Spread the nuts on a baking sheet and toast in the oven for 10 to 15 minutes, until golden brown.

For sesame seeds: Heat a dry stainless-steel sauté pan or skillet over medium-high heat for 2 minutes. Place the seeds in the skillet in a single layer and toss constantly for 45 seconds to 1 minute, until fragrant, golden brown (for white seeds), and shiny.

For cumin seeds: Heat a dry stainless-steel sauté pan or skillet over medium-high heat for 2 minutes. Place the seeds in the skillet in a single layer and toss constantly for 30 to 40 seconds, until fragrant.

peeling and seeding tomatoes

Bring a saucepan of water to a boil and score the bottom of the tomatoes with an X. Blanch the tomatoes in the water for 15 seconds and remove with a slotted spoon. When cool enough to handle, peel and seed the tomatoes.

clarified butter

Makes about 3/4 cup

Clarified butter has a rich flavor and is ideal for high-temperature cooking as it has a higher smoking point than regular butter. It is made by heating butter so that the water content evaporates and the milk solids can be separated from the butterfat (and discarded).

Chop 8 ounces of unsalted butter and melt in a heavy saucepan over medium-low heat. Cook for 3 to 4 minutes, without stirring, until the solids are separated from the clear butter liquid and are in a layer at the bottom of the pan. Gently skim off any foam from the surface and carefully pour the clear butter off into a storage container; do not let any of the solids out of the pan. Discard the solids.

sectioning citrus fruit

With a sharp paring knife, cut about ½ inch off each end of the fruit and peel off all the skin and bitter white pith. Separate each segment and peel off the membrane covering each one. Use the peeled sections or cut them to the desired thickness.

glossary

Bean thread noodles

Also called glass noodles, cellophane noodles, or saifun. A thin, clear noodle made from the starch of the mung bean. Although bean thread noodles have little flavor of their own, they soak up other flavors very well. They are sold in clear cellophane or plastic packages at Chinese or Asian markets.

Bok choy

Also known as Chinese white cabbage or pak choy. Bok choy is a cruciferous vegetable with dark green leaves and long white stems. May be substituted with the slightly smaller choy sum, or with spinach.

Bonito flakes

A Japanese seasoning made with flakes of dried mackerel. It is used as a base for dashi and other flavored broths and stocks in Japanese cooking, and sometimes as a garnish. It is usually sold in small cellophane packets at Japanese or Asian markets.

Coconut milk

A rich liquid made from grated fresh coconut meat combined with hot water and squeezed through a filter. It can be made fresh, but good-quality coconut milk is readily available in canned form.

Daikon

A large white Asian radish with crisp, juicy flesh and a fairly mild flavor. Often used in Japanese cuisine. The larger ones can be fibrous, so I recommend purchasing smaller ones (less than a pound).

Daikon sprouts

Delicately spicy sprouts of the Japanese radish (see above), with light green stems and small leafy tops. A great addition to salads and as a garnish. Interchangeable with kaiware sprouts. Daikon sprouts (or "spice sprouts") are sold in the produce section of Asian markets and some health-food stores.

Dashi

A distinctively flavored Japanese soup and stock base made primarily with kombu (kelp), dried bonito flakes, and water.

Dried shrimp

Small, dehydrated shrimp are an important flavoring and seasoning in many Asian cuisines. They are typically rehydrated in water and used whole, in chopped or minced form, or ground to form a paste. Cooking dried shrimp mellows their pungency, but they lend intensity to all kinds of fish and seafood dishes. Buy dried shrimp at Asian markets; they should have a pink or orange hue. Grayish-colored dried shrimp are likely to be less fresh. Store in an airtight container.

Edamame

Fresh green soybeans are a unique vegetable in that they are a complete protein, containing all eight essential amino acids. Their Japanese name means "beans on branches," and they are harvested while the pods are still soft, before they get a chance to harden. Edamame are enjoyed in Hawaii as a nutritious snack as well as a vegetable dish or salad ingredient. They are sold fresh, or frozen, both in the shell and in shelled form. I recommend buying frozen peeled edamane as they are easier to use.

Enoki mushrooms (enokitake)

Miniature Japanese mushrooms with slender white stalks and tiny caps. Enokis grow in clumps and are sold this way; the spongy ends should be trimmed away. Enokis have a delicate flavor and crunchy texture. They are usually sold in 3-ounce, vacuum-sealed packages.

Fermented black beans

Cooked, salted black soybeans that have been fermented; a popular ingredient in Chinese cooking. Soak the beans in water for 5 minutes to reduce their saltiness, and then rinse and drain. Fermented black beans pair particularly well with vegetables like broccoli and asparagus.

Fish sauce

A seasoning and condiment popular in Southeast Asian cooking. It is a pungent, salty, brown liquid, made from anchovies or other small fish fermented in brine. Its saltiness can be balanced and mellowed by adding sugar to the recipe. It will keep indefinitely, even unrefrigerated. I recommend nam pla, the Thai version, or patis, from the Philippines.

Furikake

A Japanese dried seasoning blend containing dried bonito flakes, ground sesame seeds, crumbled dried seaweed, and salt. It is usually packaged in small glass jars.

Ginger juice

An ideal form of ginger when you want the flavor but not the fibrous texture. Simply place peeled fresh ginger in a garlic press and squeeze over a bowl to collect the juice. Alternatively, use a juicer to extract the juice from peeled fresh ginger, or mince or grate fresh ginger and squeeze with your hand (placing the ginger in a piece of cheesecloth makes this easier).

Hoisin sauce

A sweet, spicy, and garlicky sauce made from fermented soybean paste, garlic, sugar, vinegar, and seasonings. Hoisin sauce is a popular flavoring in Chinese cooking and it can be found bottled in the Chinese section of most supermarkets, or in Chinese or Asian stores. Refrigerate after opening.

Japanese short-grain rice

At Roy's, this is the typical accompaniment with fish main course dishes. Japanese short-grain rice is starchier than the long-grain rice favored in Chinese cooking, and it is a little stickier and chewier. It is available in most supermarkets under various brand names, such as Calrose. Note that sometimes, it may be labeled "medium grain."

Kabayaki sauce

Kabayaki sauce, made with soy sauce, sugar, and mirin, is often served with eel (unagi) at sushi bars. It is available in small plastic containers at Asian stores or in the Asian condiment section of larger supermarkets.

Kaffir lime leaves

The dark green leaves of the kaffir lime tree (a citrus native to Thailand) have a strong floral-lemon fragrance and wonderful citrusy quality. Available in fresh, frozen, dried, and powdered form. I prefer to use fresh or frozen leaves. If using whole dried leaves, soak in warm water for about 20 minutes before using and remove from the food before serving (like bay leaves). Grated lime zest is the closest substitute.

Ko chu jang

Korean chile paste typically used for seasoning and as a dipping sauce or marinade. Available in Korean or Asian markets.

Kombu seaweed

Sun-dried giant sea kelp, used for flavoring dishes in Japanese cooking, including dashi and sushi. It is sold in cellophane bags at natural foods stores as well as Japanese markets and should be stored in a cool, dry place.

Lemongrass

A fragrant and fibrous stalk frequently used in Thai and other Southeast Asian cooking for its lemony, aromatic quality. The tough outer layers of the stalk should be peeled and all but the white base cut off and discarded. Lemongrass is also available in dried form. Grated lemon zest is the closest substitute.

Lop chong

A type of dried Chinese sausage that dates back thousands of years, originally made with goat and mutton meat. It has a sweet flavor and a slightly oily texture. Store in a plastic package. Keeps for months, refrigerated.

Mascarpone

A rich, buttery triple-cream cheese from northern Italy that is soft in texture and delicately flavored. It is used in savory as well as sweet dishes. You can find it in good supermarkets or Italian markets.

Maui onions

These sweet, moist, mildly flavored white onions are grown in Kula, the "upcountry" region of Maui, at an elevation of 3,000 to 5,000 feet. Other types of sweet white onion can be substituted, such as Vidalia, Texas Noonday, or Walla Walla.

Mirin

A sweet, syrupy Japanese rice wine used in sauces and marinades. The alcohol content is usually burned off in cooking, leaving the sweet flavor. Although the flavor is different, you can substitute sweet sherry.

Miso

Miso, a high-protein savory flavoring staple in the Japanese kitchen, is a thick soybean paste made by salting and fermenting soybeans and rice or barley. Miso comes in a variety of colors and textures, depending on the exact ingredients and the length of fermentation. For example, white miso (*shiro miso*), made with soybeans and rice, is thick and finely textured, sweet, and mild flavored. Red miso (*aka miso*), also made with soybeans and rice but aged longer, is salty, rich, and more strongly flavored, and yellow miso (*shinsu miso*) is smooth, mild, and salty. Different types of miso are used for different purposes, and their uses range from soups, to sauces, dressings, marinades, and as a condiment. In Japan, red miso is the type most commonly used. It is packaged in plastic tubs and can be stored in the refrigerator for up to 6 months.

Nam pla

Thai version of fermented fish sauce that is relatively mild, especially compared to Vietnamese or Burmese types.

Nori

Dried thin sheets of black-green seaweed, also called purple laver. Nori is frequently used in Japanese cooking, often for wrapping sushi and crumbled as a garnish or seasoning. Toasted nori is sold as yaki nori. Large sheets (7 by 8 inches) of nori are sold in cellophane packets, or it can be bought in strip form, in plastic containers.

Ogo seaweed

A type of brown, hairlike edible seaweed that is gathered on Hawaiian beaches and also cultivated on aquaculture farms. It is used raw or blanched, and has a naturally crunchy texture. Ogo is used both as a flavoring and a garnish. It is usually sold loose in the fish section of Hawaiian markets (see Sources, page 236).

Oyster sauce

A concentrated rich brown sauce sold in bottles, used as a flavoring and condiment in Chinese cooking; it is made from fermented oysters, soy sauce, salt, and water. It should be refrigerated after opening.

Palm sugar

A coarse, honey-colored raw sugar made from palm sap, also called coconut sugar or jaggery. Palm sugar is a common ingredient in Thai and Indian cooking and is valued for its caramel-like flavor and strong sweetness. It is harvested from palm trees, like maple syrup. It is usually sold in tubs at Asian markets. The best substitute is dark brown sugar, although the flavor is different.

Pancetta

Flavorful, unsmoked Italian bacon cured with salt and spices. Pancetta is made with pork belly and rolled up into a cylinder, like a jelly roll. I like its salty quality, especially in dishes that contain compensating sweetness or acidity. It is sold at good delis or specialty foods stores.

Panko

Crisp Japanese bread crumbs, coarser than regular bread crumbs. Panko is typically used to coat sautéed or deep-fried foods to give a crunchy texture. It is usually sold in 4-ounce cellophane packages. Substitute unseasoned fresh bread crumbs.

Pickled ginger

A common Japanese condiment, typically labeled beni shoga or gari shoga. It is sliced ginger preserved in sweet rice vinegar; it natu-rally turns pink in color. Red pickled ginger, more favored in Chinese cooking, is artificially colored. It is sold in glass jars or freshly packaged in small plastic tubs in the chilled section of supermarkets or Asian stores.

Poi

A traditional Hawaiian staple, made from pounded taro root that is steamed or boiled. Poi is a purple-grayish paste that is sometimes deliberately left to ferment and thicken, giving it a sour flavor and making it an acquired taste for some. Fresh poi, on the other hand, is a blander but more palatable food for those unfamiliar with the taste. At Roy's we make our own poi and fly it to all of our mainland restaurants, where it is on all of our menus. In Hawaii, it is usually sold in 1-pound plastic bags in the produce section.

Rayu

Red-hued spicy sesame oil. Sold in small glass bottles in the Asian section of supermarkets or at Japanese or Asian stores.

Rice wine vinegar

A light vinegar made from fermented rice wine (it is also sometimes labeled as rice vinegar).

Sake

A Japanese fermented rice wine, sake actually originated thousands of years ago in China. It is usually clear, but unfiltered sake is also available. Sake is like a dry white wine, but with much less acidity. Roy's restaurants have recently developed their own private-label line of sakes, marketed as Y brand sake. Packaged in stylish bottles, there are several types of Y sake: Wind, Sky, Rain, and Snow.

Y Wind: A dry sake, and delicately perfumed. Intense, rich flavor with a long finish.

Y Sky: Lighter on the palate but still intense in flavor.

Y Rain: Ginger-flavored sake with a clean, balanced flavor.

Y Snow: A refined, layered flavor with good intensity and balance.

Salt

Salt is the most basic of ingredients in cooking, enhancing the natural flavors of food and providing a textural element. The finely textured table salt is the saltiest choice, while the coarser kosher salt crystals have a less intense saltiness and a clean flavor. Sea salt is usually coarser still and sometimes flaky, giving a crunchy texture and mineral tones. In Hawaii, salt evaporated from sea water has been a tradition for centuries. Hawaiian sea salt has a coarse hard texture; alaea salt, which is colored with a little red earth, is a little less salty than the plain white form.

Sambal oelek

A flavorful type of Indonesian spicy chile paste containing vinegar, garlic, and brown sugar. Substitute another type of sambal (such as sambal sekera), sriracha (see below), Chinese Lan Chi chile paste with garlic, Lingham's, or other garlic chile paste.

Sambal sekera

Spicy chile paste flavored with garlic from Indonesia or Malaysia. Available bottled, in Asian stores.

Sesame oil

The dark variety is intensely flavored and aromatic oil pressed from toasted sesame seeds. Also called Asian or toasted sesame oil. Light sesame oil is a neutral, light-colored oil with a high smoking point made from untoasted seeds.

Shichimi

Japanese seasoning blend and table condiment, also labeled shichimi togarashi or hichimi. Literally "seven spices," shichimi usually contains poppy seeds, orange peel, sesame seeds, dried seaweed, pepper, and chile powder.

Shiitake mushrooms

Brown Japanese mushrooms (also known as golden oak mushrooms) with meaty caps and woody stems, available both fresh and dried. Dried shiitake mushrooms should be rehydrated before use. Now cultivated widely in the United States.

Shiso

An aromatic heart-shaped herb with serrated edges, also called perilla leaf or beefsteak leaf. Its unique, cleansing, and refreshing mintlike flavor is popular in Japanese cuisine and goes well with many types of fish. Substitute fresh basil or mint.

Soy sauce

Soy sauce is the most popular and most widely used Asian seasoning. A salty brown sauce made with soybeans, flour, salt, and water, it is available in many varieties, with different levels of saltiness and different flavors; my preference is the milder Yamasa brand for fish, and Kikkoman (a little denser and saltier) for other foods. The most important considerations when buying soy sauce are that it is naturally brewed, and that it contains no caramel as an ingredient. Shoyu is a Japanese variety often used in Hawaii that is slightly sweeter and less salty than regular soy sauce, and a little more refined in flavor.

Sriracha

A sweet and spicy Thai condiment made with chiles, tomatoes, vinegar, sugar, and salt. Sriracha is often set out on the tables of Vietnamese and Thai restaurants in a clear plastic squeeze bottle with a green top.

Taro
A nutritious tuber and staple food of ancient Hawaiian culture. Traditionally used to make poi, a starchy edible paste. The leaves can be used to wrap foods for cooking. Taro should not be eaten raw, as it may irritate the skin and throat. Substitute potatoes for the root, or spinach for the leaves.

Tatsoi
A crisply textured salad green, also known as flat cabbage. The shiny leaves are lollipop shaped and are often included in mesclun mixes; tatsoi also makes an attractive garnish.

Teriyaki sauce
Teriyaki is a thick soy-based sauce or marinade that is sweet as well as salty; in Japanese cooking it is often used for meat and poultry, as well as for fish. My easy recipe appears on page 223.

Thai chiles
All chiles are native to the Americas, and shortly after Western contact with the New World, chiles were introduced by explorers and traders around the globe. Fresh red and green Thai chiles, favored in Southeast Asian cuisines, are medium-hot, measuring about 1½ inches long and ¼ inch in diameter. Substitute fresh Serrano chiles.

Thai curry paste
There are many types available in plastic tubs at Asian markets or at some supermarkets. All types contain a complex balance of ingredients that include garlic, lemongrass, galangal, shrimp paste, kaffir lime leaves, and spices. The most common forms are green curry paste, the hottest, made with green chiles; red curry paste, made with dried red chiles; and yellow curry paste, the mildest, made with yellow chiles. Once opened, store in an airtight container in the refrigerator; do not freeze, as curry pastes tend to taste better when thawed.

Tobiko caviar
Flying-fish roe, orange in color and with a mild, sweet, fishy flavor and crunchy texture. Typically used for garnish. Substitute with masago (smelt roe), tarako (cod roe), or ikura (salmon roe). Green tobiko is tobiko flavored with wasabi.

Wakame seaweed
A type of edible flat green seaweed popular in Japan, available fresh or in dried form at Asian markets. It is typically added to soups (especially miso soups) and salads. If using dried wakame, rehydrate in warm water.

Wasabi
A hot, spicy green paste that usually accompanies Japanese sushi and sashimi, as well as other foods. Also known as Japanese horseradish, wasabi is available as a powder or as a ready-made paste. Fresh wasabi root should be peeled and finely grated.

Wonton wrappers
Very thin round or square sheets of dough made with wheat flour and egg. Typically used to make dumplings, they can be cut into strips and fried for an attractive garnish.

Yuzu
Japanese citron, a citrus fruit used for its aromatic rind and sour but flavorful juice. Available in bottled form as well as fresh at Asian markets. If unavailable, substitute an equal amount of freshly squeezed orange juice and lemon juice.

sources

These days, supermarkets across the country have Asian sections that contain many of the ingredients called for in this book. Many kitchen and specialty stores also sell Asian ingredients. Of course, some major cities have a Chinatown area that often includes markets from other Asian countries as well as different regions of China, and most large cities have neighborhoods with Asian markets. If you are still having problems locating ingredients, try calling your local Chinese, Japanese, or Thai restaurant to find out whether they can sell you specific items or give you advice on where you can locate them.

If you live in Hawaii, my leading recommendations for finding ingredients are as follows:

Tropic Fish
1020 Auahi Street
Honolulu, HI 96814
808-591-2936
www.tropicfishhawaii.com

For Pacific fish and seafood; dried shrimp; fresh seaweed (such as ogo) and caviar; Asian and Hawaiian produce (including luau leaves and poi); fresh herbs (including shiso); fresh vegetables; and certain grocery items (such as chile sauces, curry pastes, chile pepper water, and panko). Tropic Fish can fulfill mail orders as well as local orders.

Tamashiro Market
802 N. King Street
Honolulu, HI 96817
808-841-8047

For Pacific fish and seafood; dried shrimp; fresh seaweed (such as ogo) and caviar; Asian and Hawaiian produce (including luau leaves and poi); fresh herbs (including shiso); Asian spices; fresh vegetables; and grocery items. Tamashiro is another great local source but does not ship by mail.

Asian Grocery
1319 S. Beretania Street
Honolulu, HI 96817
808-593-8440

For produce, herbs, spices, and grocery items. Asian Grocery can ship within Hawaii but does not ship to other states.

Nalo Farms
41-574 Makakalo
Waimanalo, HI 96795
808-259-7698

For fresh herbs and greens. Dean Okimoto, owner of Nalo Farms, has been supplying Roy's for years. He specializes in Asian herbs and greens; call for shipping policy and information.

internet sources

There are two Internet sites that offer a wide range of Asian ingredients and offer shipping:

www.pacificrimgourmet.com
www.asianfoodgrocer.com

sake: a footnote

Finally, for sake, I can highly recommend my own ultra-premium brand—Y sake—that I created together with SakeOne. There are four varieties: Wind (very dry, full-bodied); Sky (semi-dry, medium-bodied); Snow (rough-filtered, softly sweet, full-bodied); and Rain (ginger-infused, semi-dry). Y sake is available in stores; for more information, visit: www.sakeone.com

index